The More You Get (
C

In order to get the most out of this book:

1. Determine to become a leader who has a positive impact on others.
2. Commit to bring meaning to your work through the ideas and insights in this book.
3. Improve your relationships with your employees and watch your bottom line grow.
4. Read all the chapters first then return to answer the questions and complete the exercises.
5. Stop and ask yourself as you read how you can apply each of these ideas with your current employees.
6. Underline key phrases and take notes on how to enhance your own professional and personal situations.
7. Explore each skill individually and practice every day. Practice is the key to success.
8. Change your daily conversations using some of the techniques in the book, note your impact on others and your results.
9. Share this book with your peers. Invite a colleague or a friend to learn these new concepts with you; it is a great way to support each other.
10. Follow the STAR Coaching Model, a guideline for positive and meaningful conversations with your employees, managers and peers.

Winning the Talent War

How to bring the Coaching Talent Solution
Into your workplace and transform it forever!

Denise Henry

Praise

Winning the Talent War brings management into the 21st century. In today's competitive and rapidly changing business environment, managers need to transform themselves into leaders that can inspire others while creating breakthrough results. Winning the Talent War provides tools and techniques that any manager can use to propel their business to the next level – a must have!

Leslie Beck
Principal and Owner, Compass Wealth Management, LLC

I have benefitted from Denise's coaching and have no doubt that her influence changed my career for the better. Denise is the facilitator who can dramatically increase your team's results as she did with mine. She has a commonsense approach that a person in a position of authority can use to grow and develop their employees while bringing in a bit of joy and happiness to a typical day.

Lisa Pakkebier
Executive Director, The Mentor Network

Finally, a book with solutions for collaborating and winning with our most valuable resource - our talent, and links these concepts to business goals and profits.

Erica Mathis
Controller, CPA Transit Center

In today's challenging and uncertain business climate having a 'secret sauce' is vital for success! Denise Henry's book, will provide you with a powerful and proven secret sauce that will create breakthrough results for yourself, your employees, and your company. A must read for all business leaders today!

Babette Zschiegner
Certified Coach, Owner of Peace with Autism

For more than a decade I have benefitted from Denise Henry's coaching leadership style and now she has captured her secrets in a easy to read business book. ***Winning the Talent War*** *is for even the best leaders who will read this and say 'Let's put this solution into practice!'*

Charles Robertson
Managing Director, AdvisorShares

Denise Henry has written an intimate, simple and inspiring book that gets to the core of what's important for managers who desire to become 'better' leaders. Through coaching with Denise, I grew personally and professionally and learned to use her coaching techniques with my employees. She taught me the power of asking questions, listening, and empowering individuals to lead. Denise has positively influenced my career and helped me become a better leader.

Vanessa Van Goethem-Piela
Director of Fund Development, Girl Scouts

The Coaching Talent Solution works! Denise coached me to find the answers and address difficult situations, to discover my innate talents as a leader and challenged me to accomplish my goals. She would be an asset to any organization who wants to develop their talent to create an extraordinary and productive work environment.

Francisca Villamil
HR Business Relations Leader, Cargill

Once you have created the talent pool to lead your organization to the next level you must continue to build the capabilities of your work force. The coaching approach will give you a crucial advantage in building a high-caliber, high performing team. This book does a great job of helping leaders understand the benefits of change and how to put the coaching solution into practice.

Shawn Church
Regional HR Manager, Panera Bread

*Talent alone will not win championships! Denise Henry enlightens us that Coaching is the 'secret sauce' to **Winning the Talent War**. Denise has mastered the art of coaching herself, and gives the gift of simple and practical coaching tools for us to become better leaders. Whether you are a coach of a team, leading an organization, or a front line supervisor, you are charged with transforming and keeping the best people. This is a must read!*

Greg Brenner
Exe. Dir. Organizational Development, University of Miami

*If I discover at least one tip in a business book that changes my paradigm and gives me a great new idea, I consider the time well spent. **Winning the Talent War** delivers these tips and so much more that I can use immediately with my team.*

Paul Ellis
President and COO Hoffbrau Steaks

Dedication

To my clients: past, present and future

♟

"All things become possible
when we open our minds and hearts
to the opportunities that coaching can bring."

—Denise Henry

CONTENTS

Introduction
It's a fact: *Managers with good coaching skills produce more-talented, productive employees and higher profitability for the company.*

- *Angle to Explore Possibilities*
- *Reach to the Future*
- *Example of a Coaching Conversation*

Acknowledge your employees

- *Appreciation*
- *Acknowledgment*
- *Focus on Strengths*
- *Be Positive*

Win the talent war by becoming a coaching leader

- *The Recipe for the Secret Sauce is now yours!*
- *Bring the Coaching Talent Solution™ to Your Workplace*

Introduction

[handwritten note: Underlining is not an acceptable typesetting procedure in this kind of book: Use Italics, n lc.]

It's a fact: *Managers with good coaching skills produce more-talented, productive employees and higher profitability for the company.*

The War for Talent is returning. You may already have seen a few skirmishes or even a full-blown battle, as employees who once seemed content with job security are now looking for new challenges and development opportunities.

Unlike the War for Talent in the 1990s, this one is more difficult due to the advent of social media and job search platforms, which place information on companies, job opportunities and career potential just a few keystrokes away.

Today, Winning the Talent War—attracting, developing and retaining talent—is more vital to a company's success than ever before. Because of the lightning-fast speed of technological change and global competition, products and processes are easily duplicated or leapfrogged. However, your company's employees—its talent—are not. They are unique to your company. With your coaching leadership, your employees become the source of your company's knowledge, productivity, profitability and competitive advantage.

This book is created for the CEOs, HR executives and managers who are seeking proven, effective ways to

Win the Talent War for their organizations. You are the corporate leaders who are working to ensure that your company has an environment where managers have the leadership tools they need to succeed, and employees feel inspired, challenged and appreciated.

Great Work Environments Make Dollars and Sense

To win the talent war, companies must create a workplace where employees have a strong identification—or "high engagement"—with the companies where they work. Highly engaged employees feel involved in their work, committed to the company and willing to focus extra energy and effort in meeting the company's goals.

High-engagement work environments are better places to work. Major studies show that they are also far more profitable. In a 2012 global study of 32,000 employees, consulting company Towers Watson found that companies with the most "sustainably engaged" employees had operating margins *three times higher* than companies with the lowest engagement scores. Results of a 2013 Gallup survey on "The State of the American Workplace," found that organizations with over nine fully engaged employees for every actively disengaged employee had *147 percent higher earnings per share* than their competitors. That is a huge financial and competitive advantage.

These studies quantify how great work environments can magnify employee performance. This is because engaged employees are more likely to develop the most innovative ideas and attract the most new customers. Their companies have encouraged employees to develop a creative, entrepreneurial spirit that allows them to quickly learn new skills and adapt to changing business conditions.

So, what is the secret behind "high engagement" work environments? It is not bringing your dog to work, having pizza parties on Fridays or installing pool tables in break rooms. What really makes the difference for employees is their relationship with their immediate managers. It is working with a manager who inspires employees to discover more capabilities than they knew they had. These are the managers who fit the description in Liz Wiseman's best-selling book, *"Multipliers. How the best leaders make everyone smarter."* She writes, "Multipliers have a rich view of the intelligence of the people around them." They have what Carol S. Dweck, Ph.D., describes in her book, *"Mindset: The New Psychology of Success,"* as a growth mentality, an ability to learn how they can fulfill their potential—and that of others around them.

This is a vital quality at a time when managers at all levels are challenged to meet new demands with fewer resources. If they can develop a "growth mindset" and "multiply" the talents of those around them, these managers and their employees will be far more capable, creative and resourceful. In short, they will be able to do "more with more," or as Liz Wiseman would say—be more productive by using more of their talents and skills.

Coaching leaders--the keys to winning the talent war

How do managers "multiply" the talents of those around them? Both the Towers Watson and Gallup studies show that highly engaged workers say their managers take a personal interest in their welfare, know their strengths and assign tasks most related to their skills. Very importantly, these managers coach them on the job and provide opportunities to learn new skills and advance.

In other words, these managers are what we call "coaching leaders." The Towers Watson, Gallup and other studies I refer to later in this book clearly show that developing a culture of coaching has a major positive impact on the success of individual managers, their employees and ultimately their organizations.

Coaching as a leadership style is relatively new: it was introduced in the corporate world in the 1990s, and only became recognized as an effective way to manage employees in the last decade. Years earlier, organizations felt that so long as employees were technically well-trained, they would produce good results. However, this singular focus left a void in overall employee growth, the ability to learn new skills, and contribute to creative solutions that help their businesses thrive in an environment of changing business needs.

*So, how do you develop coaching leaders in your organization? One effective way is to adopt the **Coaching Talent Solution™**. This is a program and process I've developed that teaches managers and leaders how to create positive change with others through the coaching approach to talent management. The Coaching Talent Solution™ includes all the skill sets you will find in this book plus the training to apply the skills to transform your workplace.*

Discover your talent "gold mine"

Coaching leaders do far more than set performance goals, give feedback and provide moral support. They create fertile soil where employees at all levels are encouraged to learn, grow and innovate. In today's competitive business environment, companies need to be skilled at tapping into the full scope and potential of the talent they already have. Companies could be sitting on a "gold mine" of talent and not know it. However, with coaching leaders throughout their organizations, companies can uncover hidden talent and support its growth and advancement. The late management guru Peter Drucker said, "The most valuable assets of the 20th-century company were its production equipment. The most value asset of a 21st-century institution, whether business or non-business, will be its knowledge workers and their productivity."

write out.

xvii

Develop superior performance and retention

Coaching leaders engage in a partnership with their employees. My own experience has proved that as clients work towards becoming coaching leaders, they are better able to uncover their employees' creative thoughts and ideas, and the more they involve their employees, the more motivated those employees become. But don't think coaching leaders are soft. They have high expectations of their people and guide them toward extraordinary results. Coaching leaders not only provide technical training, but also *involve* employees in their own career growth and direction. They provide more frequent feedback, help their people solve more challenging problems, adapt faster to changing conditions and take better actions.

The chart below shows how coaching leaders create a virtuous cycle that results in progressively greater productivity for employees and higher profitability for the company.

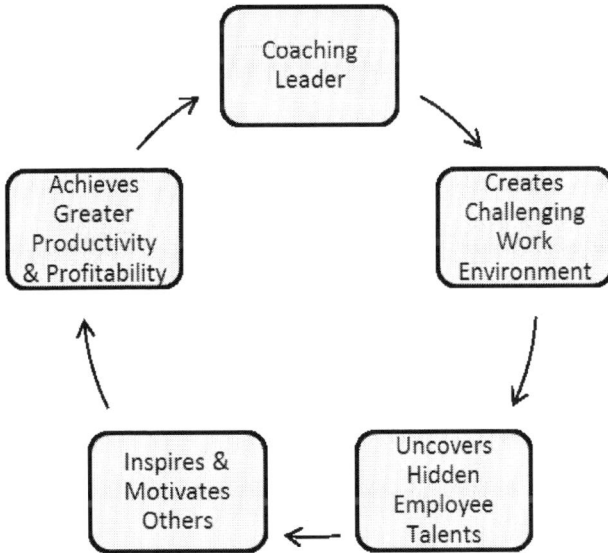

You *can* win the talent war through the Coaching Talent Solution™ that helps your managers become coaching leaders who motivate employees to be more engaged in their work and develop superior performance. A recent Zenger/Folkman survey found that employees who are managed by great coaching leaders will "go the extra mile", have improved skills and are far more likely to stay with the organization.

As an executive coach and consultant, I have the opportunity to witness the joys and frustrations my clients experience every day. My job is to support my clients as they identify their strengths, build their skills and talents and, very importantly, realize their potential. Together, we talk and walk through their unique situations and challenges to assist them in uncovering their own solutions. I help them see where they are and provide avenues to get them where they want to be as managers and emerging leaders. This book is written to help all managers who—like my clients—want to adopt a new coaching leadership style that energizes, equips and empowers employees to make meaningful contributions to the business. That is why I developed the Coaching Talent Solution™.

My goal is to help your organization:

- **Increase employee engagement**
- **Discover employees' untapped potential and creativity**
- **Improve performance**
- **Increase employees' self-motivation and self-direction**
- **Improve recruitment and retention**
- **Help managers to make the best use of their time with employees**
- **Increase its reputation as good place to work**

How do you become a coaching leader? Start Here! Read this book.

How does a manager become a coaching leader? The skills

involved aren't difficult, but they do take practice. With the help of the principles, techniques and exercises in this book, managers can learn how to make changes in their management style to become effective coaching leaders. I also provide a template for a manager's coaching conversation. I call it the STAR coaching model.

I believe this book will be very valuable in guiding managers toward becoming coaching leaders who support a positive, creative and productive work environment. Are you ready to discover your potential as a coaching leader? Let's move to Chapter One and launch our first offensive in Winning the Talent War! *discover our first stategy*

Maximizing Your Talent

Finding the "Sweet Spot"

If you are a CEO, a Human Resources executive or manager responsible for maximizing employee talent, this book could help you win the talent war, change your career...and your life.

When I begin working with my clients, I hear about their struggles to get the results they need—and expect—from their employees. Clients tell me that employees lack the same sense of urgency and understanding of how their work contributes to the business or that employees are not self-starters and require constant direction. Between the time spent on endless supervision of employees plus doing their own planning, budgeting and problem-solving, managers often feel overwhelmed and on the losing end of the talent war. They are looking for new ways to attract and retain the talent they need to meet today's objectives and be prepared for the future. To confirm comments from my clients, I did my own survey of managers, and found that:

- Some managers felt they are not equipped for long-term success.

- Many were not confident that their employees could achieve their work responsibilities.
- Most believed that overall the workforce felt dissatisfied and unfulfilled.

My survey also showed that managers often don't know how to encourage needed change in their employees. Perhaps this is because many young supervisors and managers don't get in-depth leadership training until later in their careers. However, an overwhelming 94 percent of my survey participants strongly agreed that they were anxious to adopt a different leadership style that could improve results.

proved (?)

That's why I wrote this book—to provide you, through the Coaching Talent Solution™, with the tools to adopt a coaching style of leadership that has shown to be very effective in leading and motivating employees. With this new style of leadership, managers and their companies are more likely to engage, develop and retain employees, and attract star performers. The principles in this book will help you feel more confident and fulfilled in your role as a manager, instead of wondering why your employees don't understand their part in achieving work goals.

As you develop a coaching style of leadership, you will end your work day with a sense of satisfaction instead of frustration. Very importantly, you will gain an appreciation of your employees for who they are and the jobs they do—and could be capable of— instead seeing them as a source of interruption and irritation. And your employees

2

will see you as someone who "has their back," and creates a high-energy, productive work environment.

However, winning the talent war as a coaching leader starts with _you_ and how you interact with your employees. In this book, I'll walk you through the "Coaching Style" of leadership, or "coaching leadership" for short. With an understanding and appreciation of coaching leadership, you'll be able to motivate your employees to create breakthrough results for themselves and your company. Very importantly, becoming a coaching leader could be the key to your success as a manager, the achievements of your employees, and ultimately the success of your business.

Here are just a few of the benefits and rewards you'll experience when you start using your new coaching leadership skills:

- You will step up from being a manager to also being a leader.
- Your employees will begin to think and act differently.
- Your employees will produce the results you need.
- You will feel good about yourself and your organization.
- You and your employees will have a positive impact on the bottom line.

A WINNING LEADERSHIP STYLE

By adopting the coaching style of leadership, you will discover your "sweet spot" as a manager and leader. Anyone who has played baseball or tennis is very familiar with finding the sweet spot, and its importance to winning the game. In baseball, it's hitting the ball with the part of the bat that could turn a base hit into a home run. Or in tennis, it's hitting the area on a tennis racket that converts what might have been an average serve into an ace.

In this book, we are defining **the sweet spot** as - the place where you achieve the greatest possible results with your best efforts and skills. If you believe that you aren't already operating in that optimal place, you can do what successful baseball or tennis players do—challenge yourself to find that sweet spot and improve your ability.

Take a look at the chart on the next page. There are two variables described on the chart, to reach a sweet spot:

1. Ability –your skills to perform a particular task
2. Challenge – the demand, desire and motivation to perform a task

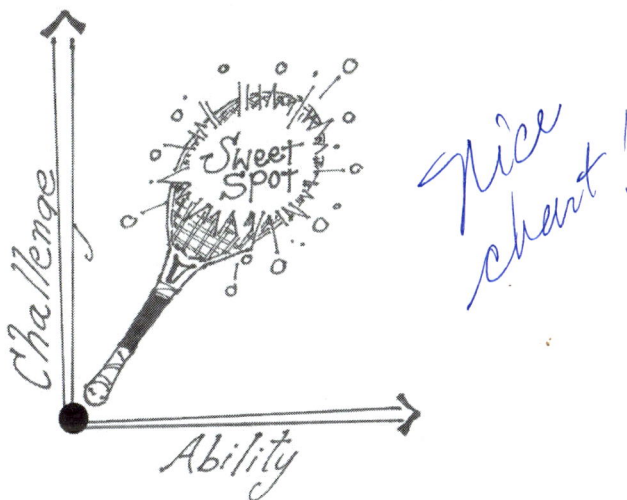

The *Sweet Spot* – your leadership ace

In the tennis racket chart above, the sweet spot is that ideal area where the challenge and your ability to meet that challenge coincide.

For instance, George is a new manager who is learning to become a coaching leader. Right now, his ability is low and the challenge of becoming a coaching leader is high. In fact, George may be feeling overwhelmed. But as he learns coaching skills, practices and continues to improve, his ability as a coaching leader will move diagonally upward toward that sweet spot. Within the sweet spot, George can achieve the greatest possible results with his employees through his best coaching efforts and skills.

When coaching leaders are in the sweet spot, they feel

confident that they have generated results for their organization by helping employees feel valued for their contributions and excited about their careers. The sweet spot is that essential area of leadership where managers make a difference for themselves, their employees and their companies.

All of us have unique gifts and talents. The key is to better understand those unique gifts and talents, and learn how to apply them in becoming a coaching leader. The late Wayman Tisdale, the number-two NBA draft pick in 1985, a three-time all-American, and an Olympic gold medal winner, is someone who found his sweet spot in leadership skills and, after his retirement from professional basketball, as a noted musician who taught himself to play the guitar. Not that any of this was easy. Tisdale's coaches benched him twice—once in college and another time in the Olympics—because he wasn't working up to his true ability. He was a natural talent but coaches felt that he needed to perfect his skills, and reach his potential. Once he found his sweet spot as a basketball player and motivator of teammates, he also was able to find his sweet spot as a talented musician. Despite the fact that Wayman, who was left-handed, had to turn his guitar upside down and restring it, he had four hit records. Wayman wasn't a coaching leader in a business sense, but he did find the sweet spot in his basketball and music careers. Like Wayman, you may need to find several new sweet spots as you move along in your career. Moving from an individual worker to a manager of staff means finding your sweet spot as a leader. Advancing further up the organization to manage managers will be a whole different ball game, as you need to find your sweet spot as a leader of leaders.

Before you became a manager, you no doubt were recognized for your individual contributions and talents, and then given the opportunity to lead others. As a manager, you are now recognized not only for your contributions, but also for having an impact through others—your employees. Your future success depends on how well you use your talents and new leadership skills to guide and motivate others.

Although you worked hard as an individual contributor, you may find that managing employees is even harder. Your employees may not share your understanding of the business and what it takes to succeed. They may very well have different attitudes, skill levels and motivators.

FORMULA FOR FINDING YOUR LEADERSHIP SWEET SPOT

Finding the sweet spot as a manager is being able to understand your employees, identify their unique talents and bring out the best in them. While I don't know of any "app" for finding the sweet spot, I do have a formula for it.

Engage + Impact + Celebrate =

Leadership Sweet Spot

To understand the formula, let's take it apart.

Engage: As a manager, to be engaged means that you are focused on growth and development of your employees, and are committed to doing what it takes to succeed. First, define what is important to you: your goals, your vision and your passion, and how you see things changing for the future that fits with your sense of meaning and purpose. (A brief pre-assessment toward the end of this chapter will help you clarify your talents and motivations.) With this awareness, you are better equipped to perform at your highest level and find solutions that have extraordinary results. While actor, writer and producer Woody Allen was quoted as saying, "Eighty percent of success is showing up," you know that a successful career as a leader is far more than a perfect attendance report. It's about challenging yourself to make a commitment – and then having the self -discipline to follow through on the necessary changes needed to reach your goals.

Impact: When you understand your goals, vision and passion, and use your best skills as a coaching leader, you will have a positive impact on employees and your organization. You will hear what your employees are really saying and work with them to develop creative solutions. When you make an impact, you contribute to something beyond yourself, by making a difference for others through your work, actions and behavior as a coaching leader.

Starting with one person at a time

A new factory manager was tasked with investigating ways to shorten production time on a manufacturing line. He could have worked on the problem himself, but instead asked line employees for suggestions. Although he was an engineer, he figured that line employees knew their own work better than he did.

Using a coaching leadership style, he involved line employees in problem-solving, figuring that they were more likely to develop a better solution, take ownership and enthusiastically implement it. In coaching conversations with employees, one line employee suggested a way to make small, but collectively significant changes to the supply lines at the factory.

Other employees noticed how enthusiastic she was about her idea and how the new manager listened carefully to her proposed solution. Soon, other employees were contributing ideas, too. As a result, the department flourished, and developed many new process improvements due to the collaborative atmosphere the new manager was creating. Everyone wanted to contribute and devote extra effort to improve productivity.

The example above shows that the changes you make by adopting the coaching style of leadership may be small at first, but they will add up. Warren Buffett of Berkshire Hathaway described his business success this way: *"I don't look to jump over seven-foot bars: I look around for one-foot bars that I can step over."*

Celebrate: To celebrate means taking the time to rejoice in what has been accomplished. Too often this step is skipped, but it is vitally important. In a 10-year, 200,000 person study of managers and employees, *Performance Accelerated: A New Benchmark for Initiated Employee Engagement, Retention and Results*, the O.C. Tanner Learning Group found organizations that recognize excellence the best have a return on equity three times higher than organizations with far less effective recognition programs. Further, 79% of employees say that lack of appreciation is an important reason they left their jobs.

Celebrating successes, the challenges you've overcome, and what you've learned from what worked and what didn't is a vital part of being an effective coaching leader. Without the "celebrate" piece of the formula, the sweet spot you've achieved is fleeting, and your employees will not receive the appreciation they deserve and the opportunity to learn from their experience. For instance, the factory manager discussed earlier made sure that the company president was aware of line employees' participation in changes to the supply line. As a result, the president attended a special recognition event for factory employees, who saw that their efforts were recognized, celebrated, and made a critical difference for the factory and the company.

This leads us back to the formula:

Engage + Impact + Celebrate =

The Leadership Sweet Spot

So how do you use your unique talents and skills to find your leadership "sweet spot"? My clients have found the following brief personal pre–assessment valuable in helping them better understand their talents and motivations. Please take a few minutes and answer the following questions.

1. What are you most passionate about?

    _____

    _____

2. What do you do best?

    _____

    _____

3. What motivates you?

    _____

    _____

add an extra line to each: there is room.

11

4. On a scale of 1 – 10, (1 considered low and 10 high), how would you rate the positive impact that you are making with your employees? What number would you like it to be and why?

_____

_____

5. How do you solve problems with employees?

_____

_____

6. What aspects of your role as a manager are you most proud of?

_____

_____

7. What would it mean to you to be able to experience greater happiness and career satisfaction as a leader?

_____

_____

8. List 4 goals or dreams you have for your business and your career.

_____

_____

9. If you could change anything about your role as a leader, what would it be right now?

_____

_____

10. How could the way your company normally celebrates successes be made more effective and motivating?

_____

_____

Now think back to your past work experiences, perhaps in a different company and a different environment. Put yourself in the position of a non-management employee.

- Did you have a sense of purpose and passion about your work? Or did you find your job draining and unproductive?
- Did employees work as collaborative teams? Or did one person do much of the work and someone else took all of the credit?
- Did you feel confident enough to take risks, or did you set safe, smaller goals, because employees were not encouraged to think outside the box?
- Were employees acknowledged for their contributions to the business, or were achievements largely ignored?
- Did you feel you were making a difference with your customers, employees, and company, or was it just business as usual day after day?

What made the difference between the best and worst

places where you've worked? If you concluded that the difference came down to leadership, you'd be in good company. In the Global Human Capital Trends 2014, published by Deloitte University Press, part of the Deloitte professional services firm, the overwhelming majority of corporate executives surveyed said that leadership is the "No. 1 talent issue facing organizations around the world."

As a coaching leader, you can bridge the leadership gap and make a positive difference for yourself, your employees and your organization.

Let's move on to Chapter Two to learn the key difference between managers and leaders.

♟

You can have everything in life you want,

if you will just help other people get what they want.

Motivation guru Zig Ziglar

Inspiring Leaders

Emerging from Management to Leadership

Business owners, CEOs, and managers from all levels tell me that the hardest part of their job is to get their employees to do what they need them to do. I'm willing to bet that when you think about finding your "sweet spot" as a leader, a major part of your focus is on your employees and how you can encourage their understanding of and commitment to achieving business goals. If your employees were all in sync—doing what you need them to do— wouldn't that go a long way to helping you find your leadership sweet spot? After all, your employees would be producing positive results, which in turn would make your work life easier and help boost your company's bottom line. Here's the good news: There is a fundamental way to change your relationship with your employees. It's all about becoming a *leader* – the best leader that you can be, which then will inspire your employees to more fully use their talents, creativity and initiative.

The key to changing your relationship with your employees is to step out of your manager role to become a leader, especially when change and innovation is needed (which seems to be all of the time these days). Management and leadership are both important in business, but have different purposes and outcomes. Managing is largely task-oriented while leading is more visionary and strategic. Being a leader who inspires and empowers employees requires a bit more time and effort, but is well worth the work involved. That's because your leadership skills will help develop employees who are more motivated and committed to achieving their goals and, ultimately, to the success of the organization.

In its 2014 Human Capital Trends survey, consulting firm Deloitte reported that corporate leaders across the world identified leadership as the most urgent business concern, with leadership gaps in every level of the organization. "In a world where knowledge doubles every year and skills have a half-life of 2.5 to 5 years, leaders need constant development," the report said. By developing new and effective leadership skills, with an ability to inspire breakthrough performance among employees, you will help your company win the talent war, and advance your own career.

Let's further explore the difference between a leader and a manager. Here's an analogy that compares the two: a manager can be thought of as the engineer of the train, while a leader determines where the train is going. This means that leaders need to *think and act* differently than managers. Leaders put a great deal of focus on their teams: they have a vision for the future of the business, develop shared goals with their employees, and motivate their people to attain them. Then leaders get out of the way so employees can use their skills and talents toward achieving those goals. Partnering and collaborating with employees will move you a lot closer to the leadership "sweet spot," rather than micro-managing.

Leadership beginnings

One of my earliest memories of leadership was being a captain of my high school drill team. Because the drill team performed during half time at basketball and football games, this was a big and visible role at my high school, especially where I grew up in Texas, where football was the state pastime. While I once focused on being the very best on the technical dance side and having a good relationship with my 40 or so team members, as a captain, I now had to share my knowledge with others so they could be their very best, too.

During performances, I never worried that we'd have problems. I just knew we were already prepared; the important work had already been done in practice. You can imagine what it was like leading a group of teenagers while being a teenager yourself. The drill team practiced early in the morning and after school, an exhausting schedule, punctuated by the usual teenage personal drama. My job as a leader was to help refocus and prioritize our energy so we'd all be in that line, in a single pose, as a group of individuals working together to create

17

a show as a team.

Take a walk down memory lane, and remember when you first noticed yourself in an emerging leadership position. Maybe it was first chair in the orchestra, captain of the baseball team or president of the marketing club. How did you transform from an individual contributor to a leader. What role did you play? How did others view you? What similar traits do you notice about yourself today?

How would those leadership traits help you in your leadership role now? Your employees come to work with all types of challenges--issues they bring from home, conflicts between co-workers, personal doubts and unrealized dreams. A leader recognizes that individuals often can't compartmentalize these issues from their work responsibilities and finds a way to rally the troops by offering direction and support so the team can refocus and work as a committed and effective group. A leader also has an important role of communicating to employees, supporting them with one-on-one time so that they may find solutions to their work issues while exploring ways to realize their potential.

Becoming a leader is as process that takes time: we start off as employees, become managers and work our way into leadership. As managers, we focus on planning and implementing, often getting caught up in details and micro-managing employees. As a result, we often don't have time to give much-needed thought to strategic planning, and helping employees understand how their work is connected to the company's goals and vision for the future.

MANAGEMENT AND LEADERSHIP

Over the years, there have been plenty of studies about the important differences between managers and leaders. Take a look at the chart below, which outlines the primary differences.

Manager	Leader
Administers	Innovates
Focuses on the present	Focuses on the future
Scrutinizes performance	Searches for potential
Performs duties	Pursues the vision
Relies on control	Inspires trust
Focuses on process	Focuses on people
Maintains	Develops
Gets people to do things	Empowers others to grow
Does things right	Does the right thing
Runs meetings	Facilitates team growth
Gives answers	Asks empowering questions

It's important to note that there are times when you will be a manager, especially when guiding a less experienced employee or implementing a new business process. At other times, you will best serve your company, customers and employees by being a leader. In today's business environment, management and leadership complement one another. Your evolution from manager to both manager *and* a leader might seem daunting at first, but your career will greatly benefit from this vital transition. Take another look at the chart, especially at the leader's column. Do you see a common thread or theme? You notice that leaders focus on their *people* more than on tasks. Don't worry if you're not as confident about being the leader you aspire to be right now; your strengths and talents can be developed as your leadership skills emerge. Finding your leadership sweet spot is where you want to be as you work toward developing a brighter future, with a positive impact for you, your team and your company to achieve the *big wins*.

**Tired of wrestling between being a manager and leader?
Become a coaching leader and everybody wins!**

LEADERSHIP *PLUS* HEART

Successful leaders operate both from their heads *and* hearts. Leaders need to use their brainpower when it comes to strategy, prioritization, and making sound decisions. These are all good skills, to be sure. But in today's business environment, people skills are a high priority as well. Study after study shows that emotional intelligence (or heart) contributes far more to a person's job success than intellect. The best business leaders must be adept at building relationships and influencing others. Many leaders adopt behaviors they've witnessed or experienced—because they think (in their heads) that's the way they're *supposed* to be—even if it doesn't feel right (in their hearts). If you adopt a style of leadership that is different from who you really are, then finding your leadership sweet spot will be all but impossible. To be the best leader you can be, add a little heart.

GUIDING PRINCIPLES

There are three guiding principles to leading with your heart:

1. Be Present

2. Be Committed to your Employees

3. Operate with Integrity

Each of these principles involves how you interact with your employees.

21

Be Present

In this multi-tasking world, it's rare for us to focus our attention on just one thing and to be fully present for that one thing. Leading from the heart requires strength and determination to do just that. You must be in the moment with your employees, fully aware. It's necessary to listen deeply, not only to what is being said by others, but to what you are feeling on the inside. To be present, you must be aware of your own feelings and emotions and learn to recognize the impact you have on others. Take your employees' thoughts, feelings and perspectives into consideration. When you cultivate this awareness by being present, you will understand where your employees are coming from and help them identify solutions and goals that will get them to where they need to be.

Be Committed

No doubt you're fully committed to bottom-line results, but that's only part of the puzzle. With any relationship, you need a high level of commitment to thrive and make it through the rough spots. Without that same level of commitment to your employees, there's a missing piece: The supportive and positive feelings for others—or the *heart* portion of leadership. Be committed to developing your employees and helping them reach their full potential. You will find that in turn they will give you their commitment to work hard towards your success, and that of your organization. Here's how to demonstrate your commitment to your employees:

- Believe in their positive intentions.

- Be open-minded, without judging.

- Be willing to see things from a new perspective.

- Allow employees to take ownership and accountability for their work.

- Focus on having open communication to avoid misunderstandings and making incorrect assumptions.

As a coach, I have certain rituals I go through to prepare for a coaching session. I begin by getting my materials together, reviewing what we did during our last session, and visualizing what we might do today. To be open to new ideas and possibilities for my clients, I have to let go of distractions, and get centered.

Certain phrases help me focus. Here are a few of my favorites.
- Let me be present.
- Everything right now is as it should be.
- I am open to all opportunities.
- I welcome this chance to be here for this person.

In the meeting with your employee, don't make assumptions – be a detective and get curious. Find out where your employee is both mentally and emotionally as you begin the conversation. Connection is the powerful first step in the coaching conversation. This is your opportunity to be able to better understand your employee and get a heightened sense of what they need and how you can support them. Then drop any expectations so that you can become a *mirror*, allowing employees to reflect on their present state to design more desirable goals and actions.

Operate with Integrity

The last guiding principle of leading with heart is operating with integrity. It's important to be true to your word and consistent with your behavior. Find out what your employees need from you, whether it is opening the door to possibilities, or the tools and training to improve performance and realize their potential. When confronting issues, be aware that your words and actions have an impact on your employees. Be sure that impact is positive.

Commit to being honest and open at all times while listening to things from your employees' point of view. When you discuss their desires and potential, let them see how their role and purpose fit into the organization's bigger picture. If your employees can trust your intentions and behaviors, they will sense your authenticity and come forward with concerns and ideas, resulting in a deeper and healthier working relationship.

Here's an exercise that will help you support and build your relationships with your employees._List your employees on the chart below. Next to their names, write one or two ways you could improve your interactions with them and one way you could show your personal commitment to their advancement.

Name	Improve interaction	Show personal commitment
1.		
2.		
3.		
4.		
5.		
6.		
7.		
8.		
9.		
10.		

Remember—Only by understanding where your employees are coming from, can you help them find where they should be going. Let's move on to Chapter Three, to begin your journey toward being the leader you want to be.

♟

Your vision will become clear only when you look into your heart.
Who looks outside, dreams.
Who looks inside, awakens.

—Psychologist Carl Jung

Engaging In Your Own Journey

Are you the leader you want to be?

Perhaps you've heard the saying, "*When you point a finger at someone else, there are three fingers pointing back at you.*" Stop for a moment and ask yourself how often you point a finger at your employees. Are there instances when your employees are at fault? Absolutely. However, blame is destructive, not constructive. It fails to recognize that most people have a natural desire to perform well, develop and grow. We're all guilty of pointing the finger from time to time. When you find yourself placing blame on your employees, it's time to take a step back and look in the mirror. To effect change in your employees, you must change yourself first.

A Moving Story

I have deservedly earned the title of Relocation Queen, who can count 28 moves in my lifetime. My parents moved us often when I was a child, and when I grew up, it continued to be a way of life for me. When the going got tough, I felt that the solution was to pack and move. Instead of looking at what I needed to change, I went straight to my "easy" solution—a change of scenery rather than a change of mindset. I needed to test my own assumptions and beliefs about what else might be possible instead of "moving" too quickly.

The LifeLaunch™ Program at The Hudson Institute was a perfect beginning for me to explore a more purposeful way of living. My coaches asked powerful questions, which allowed me to dig deep and explore my intentions and desires in life. This program showed me that my background, skills and personal goals were ideally suited for a career as a professional coach. Years later I found that I could achieve my expanded career goals by helping others achieve their goals through coaching leadership.

KNOW YOURSELF FIRST

Being a leader begins with personal leadership. If you want to lead others and, if you want to find your sweet spot as a leader, you must first be able to lead yourself. Leading yourself begins with knowing yourself and understanding your style of leading others. Most styles come naturally and are a function of your personality and competencies, including how you communicate and work with others. Some individuals are naturally people-oriented, while others are naturally task-oriented.

Your personal style of managing others creates a climate and culture within your organization. That climate may be motivating for your employees, or it may be demotivating. The climate you create will contribute to the level of staff productivity, and ultimately determine your results and stature as a leader. The key to becoming an effective leader is to be able to use the right style—or range of styles—at the right time, based upon the situation.

Before reading any further, stop and think about yourself and your personal style. Reflect on your interactions with your employees. How do you lead people?

- Are you a people-oriented person, or a task-oriented person?
- Do you prefer to get everyone in a room and make decisions together?
- Do you focus on keeping everyone happy and tend to avoid confrontation?
- Do you work long hours and expect your employees to follow in your footsteps?
- Do you have a tendency to tell others what to do and how the job should be done?

THE MOST COMMON LEADERSHIP STYLES

It's not uncommon for leaders to use a single style to manage others, and to use that style over and over, no matter the situation. Some styles overlap and can be used hand-in-hand. Other styles may be unconstructive for the situation, yielding less than desirable results. Let's take a look at the six most common leadership styles:

1. **Harmonious Style** – The harmonious leader is a true people-person who regularly creates harmony and builds emotional bonds. Positive feedback and

employee morale are focal points. The harmonious leader also is less likely to enter into difficult conversations with employees and avoids performance-related confrontation. This leadership style tends to reward the characteristics of the employee more than the performance of the employee. As a result, employees may be allowed to remain at a certain level, even though they are underperforming.

2. **Participative Style** – The participative leader is a people-person who allows employees to share in decision-making. While the leader will make the ultimate decision, consensus through participation is typically used to increase job satisfaction. This type of leader can be counted on to call frequent meetings to listen to employee concerns. This style is often used when teamwork is paramount. Negative conversations are typically avoided. This style can lead to slower decision-making, "group think," and less focus on evaluating both the positive and negative outcomes of a decision.

3. **Visionary Style** – The visionary leader communicates a future vision for the organization and brings people together around a shared sense of purpose: to achieve the vision. The visionary leader conveys a sense of commitment so that the vision becomes the stimulus for all employee activity. Visionary leaders offer a balance of

positive and negative feedback to their employees, with the intention of obtaining better results. The visionary leader is equally people-focused and task-focused, but tends not to be detail-oriented, leaving employees to "sweat the small stuff." And sometimes, "small stuff" can become "big impediments" to achieving the leader's vision later on.

4. **Pacesetting Style** – The pacesetting leader is a task-oriented, high performer. The focus is on the leader's own achievement and an expectation that others act similarly. The pacesetter leads by example and sets high standards. This type of leader finds it hard to delegate because of the belief that "no one can do it better." Employees who haven't demonstrated high performance in the past will most likely not be provided with opportunities to grow and develop. The pacesetting leader does not tolerate poor performance and responds by micro-managing.

5. **Directive Style** – Directive leaders are task-oriented individuals who are all about results...as long as the results are achieved their way. This leader gives orders and expects those orders to be followed. "Controlling" and "micro-managing" are words used to describe the directive leader. For example, this style can be helpful for a manager of

employees who are new in their positions, when projects have changed or the company has a new strategic direction. Such leaders use dominant guidance and direction to avoid confusion about the expected behaviors and outcomes.

6. **Coaching Style** – The coaching leader is focused on nurturing skills, developing talent and inspiring results with their employees. The coaching leader spends time in conversations that focus on the future, exploring possibilities and new behaviors. In coaching conversations with the leader, employees develop goals, plan actions and agree upon results to be accomplished within a specific time frame. They allow employees freedom to use their creativity to meet those performance goals and deadlines.

I suspect you recognize yourself in one or more of the above leadership styles. I certainly do.

What training a puppy taught me about leadership!

Four years ago, I adopted Misty, a half beagle, half Basset Hound mix. My goal was to create the perfect companion for my family, eager to play and take walks while leaving our floors and carpets free of puppy accidents. Prior to Misty, I thought I was so evolved as a coach. But this puppy was determined to be my match. She chewed our shoes and had frequent accidents. I spent many days holed up in my office and kitchen where her accidents would do the least damage. I spent most of my time correcting her and, as a result, she lay in the corner, looking me with those big, sad Basset Hound eyes. In essence, I was the typical micromanager. A friend who is also a coach listened to my trials with Misty and told me I was not being my caring and positive self with the dog. "You're not having fun with her. You're spending way too much time waiting for her to do something wrong," she said. I always told my clients that coaching skills applied not only to employees but also friends and family members. Maybe it applied to dogs, too. So I took Misty outside and played with her—a lot. I rewarded her when she did her "business" outside, and when she sat and heeled on command. As a result, Misty learned that I was a source of fun and praise, someone she was anxious to please. Indeed, coaching has wider applications than I imagined. That said, I am not the person to come to for suggestions about training your dog.

Exercise: Test your understanding of each of the leadership styles. (Exercise key is located at the end of the chapter.)

Match a leadership style with each of the following scenarios.

1. Harmonious Style   2. Participative Style

3. Visionary Style   4. Pacesetting Style

5. Directive Style   6. Coaching Style

A._____ Henderson began a new division of his demolition company that reclaims old wood. He sought out like-minded people to build furniture solely made from reclaimed wood. He often chooses workers committed to green living over more qualified applicants who don't share the same vision.

B._____Peterson won the top salesman award for 10 straight years before he became a manager. He promotes weekly, monthly, and annual challenges with bonuses, awards for the winners and demotions for losers.

C. _____Bronson encourages teamwork and participation in group activities designed to increase harmony and morale. He plans employer-sponsored outings and events. His desire to avoid conflict can leave underperforming employees on

34

his team and higher performers unrecognized for their efforts.

D._____Turner began her company after leaving the Marines. She gives clear and concise directions and expects them to be followed. She tries to be involved in all areas of the business and believes in direct comments when things begin to go wrong.

E._____ Ellis has a personal and business-growth mindset. She focuses on possibilities and encourages her employees to explore opportunities for advancement. She makes time to talk and connect with employees. Ellis routinely celebrates accomplishments on the way to breakthrough performance.

F._____Clarkson is famous for her staff meetings. There's an inside joke that donuts can't be ordered without group consensus. She has an open door policy and a perennially positive attitude. Decision-making can be slow, dissention is discouraged and there is less focus on potential negative outcomes of a decision.

Peter Drucker recognized that changes in the business world would require managers to not only maximize efficiency but also to nurture employee skills, develop talent and inspire results. He wrote, "The task is to lead people. And the goal is to make productive the specific strengths and knowledge of every individual."

The harmonious, participative, directive, visionary and pacesetting leadership styles may be appropriate at times, but when used exclusively, they can lead to undesirable results. The coaching style of leadership has broader application in today's business environment of rapid change and globalization.

As a coaching leader, you can help your employees build their creativity and talent, which benefits them, you and the organization. Your employees will be less dependent on you, freeing your time to be more visionary and expand your own knowledge and skills. Collaborating with employees is far more satisfying than micro-managing them. Adopting the coaching style helps you to move up from being a manager to being a manager *and* a leader with heart. Becoming a coaching leader holds the key to finding your sweet spot as a leader. It's also the key to your future and the future of your business. (It's the "secret sauce".) In Chapter Four, you'll discover more about the "secret sauce" and the benefits of using the coaching style.

Exercise Key: A -3   B - 4   C-1   D-5   E-6   F-2

When you look in the mirror, who do you see?

♟

I'm starting with the man in the mirror.
Take a look at yourself and then make a change.

—Writers and composers Glen Ballard and Siedah Garrett

♟

How do you go from where you are to where you want to
be?
You have to have an enthusiasm for life.
You have to have a dream, a goal, and
you have to be willing to work for it.

—Former College Basketball Coach Jim Valvano

Chapter Four

Creating Impact to Retain and Attract the Best Talent

Coaching—it's the secret sauce

"I have so much on my plate right now. The last thing I need is spending time hand-holding my people."

"I'm frustrated and tired: I put so much time and effort into this company, but I can't get things to improve."

"This job just isn't fun anymore, and my stress level is off the charts."

Do any of the above comments resonate with you? These are a sampling of remarks I hear over and over from my clients. In working with managers, I've observed that their challenges typically are **perceived as** employee problems and/or not enough time. These challenges result in frustration and stress. The solution? Become a coaching leader. It's the "secret sauce" to winning the talent war. And having a "secret sauce" (for Texas barbecue) is second only to football in my home state.

HOW COACHING IMPACTS YOUR BUSINESS

I guarantee that the time you spend learning and adopting the coaching style of leadership will be more than offset by the time you save later as your employees become more self-directed and productive. As a leader, you face a multitude of challenges, and I believe the coaching style of leadership can help with many of them. For example:

Developing and retaining qualified employees — Many businesses invest thousands of dollars to hire and train a new employee. Employee retention is vital to the long-term success of your business. There are numerous ways to retain your best employees, and one of the most fundamental is supporting them in developing new skills. The more you help your employees learn and grow, the more likely they will be fully committed to their work, you and the company. Through adopting a coaching style, you will help your employees be more productive and ready to take on new work challenges. In addition, through continuing one-on-one conversations with your staff, you will find that coaching is the perfect tool to help identify employees who are the best fit with your group or organization and those whose skills might be more suited for another department or company. By coaching, you get a heads up well in advance about performance challenges and can manage the transition of work responsibilities from one employee to another. Through coaching, you can manage talent moving in, out and around your company.

Measuring performance — Here's a business adage, but it's true: "What gets measured gets *managed.*" I sometimes find that my clients *assume* there's a mutual understanding of employees' roles, responsibilities and work goals. We all know what happens when we assume: assumptions result in breakdowns. Setting specific and measurable goals with an employee is part of coaching. When you adopt a coaching style, assumptions are replaced by clarity so that you and the employee are not working at conflicting purposes.

Motivating employees — To motivate means *to give incentive to.* Inherent in the coaching style is much improved employee motivation. Studies have shown that employee job satisfaction is directly associated with the relationship an employee has with his or her boss. The coaching style helps you to develop a positive relationship with each of your employees. People are incentivized when they feel heard, cared about and treated as individuals.

Improving productivity — Intrinsic to the coaching style is setting mutually agreed-upon goals and tracking performance to reach those goals. Coaching is the way to help support your employees' performance. It helps to increase employee focus and skill level, contributing to productivity improvement.

Recruiting quality employees — A survey conducted in October of 2012 by Right Management, a global leader in talent and career management workforce, indicates that there is considerable job dissatisfaction throughout North America. Manpower CEO Owen J. Sullivan remarked "the levels of discontent we're now finding have to be without precedent." Employee turnover is costly. However, adopting a coaching style of leadership results in a culture of growth and development, making your organization more attractive to both current and potential employees.

Time management — Managers typically wear a multitude of hats and are forced to multi-task. Often, they're so busy putting out day-to-day fires that they have little time to focus on the important, longer-term activities that will move the business forward. When I talk with my clients about placing a greater focus on their employees, I often hear, "I don't have time for that. I don't have time to sit and talk with my employees one-on-one." However, because there are so many benefits to adopting a coaching style, you will be rewarded immensely for finding the time to have coaching sessions with your staff. You may not have as many fires to put out, your employees will be more productive and the truly vital work of your organization will get done as a result.

How Coaching Transformed an Employee's Career – and Mine, too

Early in my career, I worked as a training manager in a financial services firm, where Matt was a superstar brokerage representative. Matt was rewarded for his performance with a promotion to trainer for his department. Matt may have exceeded all expectations when it came to being a broker, but he certainly didn't exceed management's expectations as a trainer. In fact, he struggled in the new position and his performance reviews were abysmal.

When the training department was reorganized, Matt was moved to my team. "Handling the problem," (i.e., Matt) was now my job. I was regarded as a good manager and thought that my gentler, more flexible management approach would help turn Matt's performance around. Telling him what to do and reprimanding him had not worked for his previous managers. Unfortunately, despite my best efforts, Matt's poor performance continued. I had tried everything in my management "arsenal" and reached my wits' end. Human Resources' solution was to put Matt on probation, but my instinct told me there had to be a better way.

Fortunately, a colleague suggested that coaching, which was just in its infancy at the time, might help. I did some research and decided to give this thing called coaching a try. In my heart, I wanted to help Matt by learning what was behind his performance issues, and open up some new possibilities for him. Was it feasible to use coaching to improve Matt's performance, and help the company to retain a smart and talented person at the same time? I was determined to find out

In my research, I found that one of the basic principles of being a coaching leader is becoming a good listener, so I decided it was my time to listen to Matt and better understand him. In our meeting, I discovered that no one had asked Matt how he felt about the promotion or what his real career aspirations were. In fact, no one had even asked him if he wanted to become a trainer. He was just promoted into a position that was not a good fit for his strengths. (It was an obvious case of using neither head and nor heart in making this unfortunate management decision.)

Ultimately, Matt understood that he strengths were not suited for the training position, but knew he had to improve his performance before he could apply for another job in the organization. He didn't know how to do that, which was extremely frustrating for him and a source of his poor performance. Matt and I agreed on steps he could take to improve as a trainer, and how I could support him going forward. Having a powerful new vision for his future, Matt was inspired to put in the extra work. That meeting was the beginning of a changed relationship between Matt and me.

What I didn't know then was that it was the spark that eventually would launch me on a new career path – as executive coach, consultant, author, and developer of the Coaching Talent Solution™.

But back to Matt - The day came when Matt moved to a different department where he once again became a superstar. From then on, I was sold on the concept of coaching leadership as an effective management style. Adopting a coaching style allowed me to break through barriers, help an employee improve his performance and save a good employee for the organization. I knew that being a coaching leader was the solution I'd been looking for when it came to adopting the right style of managing and motivating others.

I also found that the coaching leadership style is not only for struggling, challenged employees, but also for strong performers who want to grow and develop their careers. If strong performers see potential for advancement and are also challenged and recognized, chances are good that they will remain with the organization. This is where coaching leaders can positively impact retention of key employees – and establish themselves as highly effective managers who can influence and motive others.

ENGAGING YOUR EMPLOYEES

The coaching style of leadership differs from all other styles in that coaching leaders show that they care about their people *and* establish collaborative partnerships with them.

For a number of years, coaching has been identified as the one leadership style that results in increased productivity with employees. Why? Because coaching leaders engage their employees. According Towers Watson's Managing Director Julie Gebauer, engagement "measures the level of connection employees feel with their employer, as demonstrated by their willingness and ability to help their company succeed, largely by providing discretionary effort on a sustained basis." In the Towers Watson global workforce study mentioned earlier, it was found that employees are actually eager to invest more of themselves (i.e., put in more time and effort) to help their company succeed. Employee engagement these days, however, is an endangered species. Following are more results of the Towers Watson global workforce study:

- Barely one in five employees (21%) are engaged on the job.
- Eight percent are fully disengaged.
- The remaining 71% fall into two categories: Enrolled (partially engaged) and Disenchanted (partially disengaged).

- There is a clear connection between engagement and retention. The more engaged the workforce, the greater the percent of employees who plan on staying with their current employer.
- Organizations should continually assess and measure engagement levels.

But here's the good news: if you and your company succeed at engaging employees, you have an important competitive advantage over companies who don't. As you learn to become a coaching leader, chances are that you will find employees with untapped potential who *want* to be more involved, and help their company succeed. In order for them to help you, you must first help them. Coaching leaders work together with their employees to discover hidden potential.

An employee's hidden potential

A few years ago, I worked with Troy, a frustrated human resources manager. He found a passion and a gift for creating solutions for organizational development issues, but that wasn't his label. He felt stuck in a job managing benefits and compliance issues. When he suggested creative solutions in business meetings, he was ignored since this wasn't his official area of expertise.

Troy searched out articles and books about different companies that changed their business culture and improved their bottom lines. He spoke to his boss offline about his research, but was ultimately ignored. Troy volunteered to facilitate team-building exercises and to design leadership training programs; however, management discounted his ideas for the programs because it required too much change in how they saw Troy as an employee.

As his coach, I worked with Troy to discover his vision for the future, and helped him create a plan for him to realize his goals in spite of the obstacles that he faced. He was convinced that he had the talent for organizational development (OD) work but had no idea how to make the job change happen. He enrolled in in a nationally recognized program and became certified as an OD consultant at his own expense, working after hours and on the weekends.

He left the company to become Vice President of Organizational Development in a more prestigious, successful organization that was grateful to benefit from his skills. His former company lost a valuable asset because management couldn't get beyond his job title to see his hidden talent.

The most successful companies and managers look at the interests, skills, and untapped abilities of employees and encourage their growth. If they don't, they may be on the losing side of the war for talent.

CREATING A COMPETITIVE ADVANTAGE

When you become a coaching leader, you create a competitive advantage. As you embrace and adopt the coaching style of leadership, the culture of your organization will begin to change. A coaching culture drives performance. Coaching will result in more engaged employees who enjoy their work and want to make a contribution to the business. Ultimately, engaged employees result in more satisfied customers. The benefits of becoming a coaching leader are substantial. Your employees will:

- Fully participate in their work, as opposed to just doing the minimum.
- Want to be held accountable for what they aspire to develop or produce.
- Feel connected, valued and listened to.
- Partner in the success of the business, finding personal success in the process.
- Have increased confidence and competence.
- Contribute innovative ideas and solutions.
- Become engaged and therefore less likely to leave the company.
- Have stronger, trusting relationships with you as their manager.
- Align their goals with your goals and those of the organization.

Does it sound like adopting a coaching style is the be-all and end-all? As my clients have discovered, it's close. I'm convinced you'll be thrilled with the results of being a coaching leader. You will be glad that you now have the special ingredient for that secret sauce for success as a manager—the coaching style of leadership.

♟

If your actions inspire others to dream more, learn more, do more and become more, you are a leader.

—Former U.S President John Quincy Adams

Chapter Five

Developing Your Employees with Coaching

A pathway to transformation

Coaching positively transforms the culture in any business: When you become a coaching leader, you move from a focus of "what's best for the business" to "what's best for the business *and* what's best for the employees." The coaching leader establishes a collaborative partnership with employees, often centered on achieving goals that are more aligned with the personal and professional aspirations of the employee and the vision of the organization. A coaching leader supports, guides and challenges employees to reach their full potential. This is done by having one-on-one conversations with employees, resulting in some out-of-the-box thinking and ultimately breakthrough results. (In Chapter Nine, I will provide you a four-step model for a coaching conversation.)

PERFORMANCE, GROWTH AND MOTIVATION

Coaching conversations are two-way, not one-way. These conversations are very different from other communication approaches in which you, as the manager, tell your employees what to do. When you adopt the coaching style of leadership, you engage your employees in not only improving performance but also in conversations about how to:

- Create learning opportunities.
- Find new solutions.
- Contribute in more effective ways.
- Achieve happiness and fulfillment at work.

Coaching conversations result in discovering the hidden potential your employees have to offer. The result is employee growth and improved performance. Additionally, the coaching style provides plenty of opportunities for you to acknowledge and appreciate your employees, thus increasing motivation. And you will find that it works with friends and family, helping to improve relationships with employees and loved ones—even teenagers!

Going Back to School

As our daughter was about to start middle school—a scary time for any parent--my husband and I wanted to have a quality conversation with her, hoping to help her ease the transition from elementary school. We asked her about her concerns about middle school and found that most of her worries focused on meeting people and making connections. We told her stories about our experiences at the same age and she later told us stories about her initial days at middle school.

*One day, early in the school year, a group of her new friends asked if she could join them at a carnival two towns over. To us, this sounded like a big step for our young daughter, who would be by herself with new friends in an unfamiliar place. So, we asked her what she wanted and what she thought was the best decision. Ultimately she decided that she would **not** go, feeling unprepared for that level of independence at the time.*

By listening, we were able to understand her concerns. Without giving opinions and possibly creating embarrassment, we were able to listen so that she could have the courage and strength to make her own decision. She wasn't looking for us to give her advice; she was looking for us to listen.

CAREER DEVELOPMENT

As a leader, you can use coaching conversations not only to grow your employees in their current jobs, but to create open dialogue about where they see themselves in your organization in the future. These conversations engage your employees in expanding the scope of what's possible for their future development. Coaching conversations invite employees to...

- Share their thoughts about current job satisfaction.
- Tell you how they hope to partner with the company going forward.

- Be mindful about their current skills and competencies, and identify purposeful steps toward building their careers.
- Take appropriate actions to accomplish their long-term goals.

Change is a process and it just takes...action.

FEEDBACK VERSUS COACHING

Feedback and coaching are offered to employees with the identical goal in mind: to help employees grow and develop in their positions, thereby improving their performance. We tend to think of feedback as negative, but it can also be positive. Giving praise is a form of feedback that reinforces positive behavior and encourages an employee to continue that behavior. On the other side of the equation, feedback can be used when an employee engages in an undesirable behavior. However, the coaching leader provides information that helps employees redirect their performance in a positive and respectful way.

Take a look at the chart below to understand the difference between feedback and coaching:

Feedback	Coaching
Offers an observation about a behavior	Explores *new* behaviors
Brief, timely, focused on what just happened	Future-focused, longer conversation
3 parts: a. behavior observed b. impact of the behavior c. change that must be made	Exploring solutions

Managers Often Think They're Coaching When They're Not

A few years ago, I was meeting with a new client, Kevin, a company president. During our conversation, *Kevin told me he was already using what he believed to be a coaching style with his employees and, in fact, he had just coached one of his managers, Christina, that morning. Kevin told me he had invited Christina to his office to discuss her multiple missed days of work and tardiness in the past month. However, Kevin never actually asked what was going on in her life to cause the missed work days and lateness. Instead, he told Christina he would not tolerate her being late for work or calling in sick. Christina apologized and agreed she would work hard to remedy the situation. Kevin thanked Christina, made some small talk about her family, and then Christina went back to her desk.*

Kevin viewed this encounter with Christina as coaching because he cited "the problem," and she said she would change. Then—in his mind—he softened the blow by making small talk before Christina went back to her desk. Take another look at the table above, and you'll see that Kevin was not coaching Christina. Rather, he was providing feedback. Had Kevin wanted to coach Christina, he would have had a different conversation, a true, two-way conversation in which he asked Christina questions about *her* thoughts and concerns in addition to exploring new behaviors, obstacles that might be in the way, and ways to improve her attendance going forward.

BEING COMPASSIONATE

The coaching leader brings an aspect of caring to the manager-employee relationship. Coaching is a positive and motivational style that includes heart, an often-elusive aspect of leadership. Using the guiding principles of leading with your heart is all about caring for and building relationships with your employees.

A study by Dale Carnegie Training found that a key motivator for employee engagement is a strong relationship with the immediate supervisor, echoing similar findings by Gallup and Towers Watson mentioned earlier. The Dale Carnegie white paper, *What Drives Employee Engagement and Why It Matters*, (2012), summarizes the results of this study, and indicates that caring managers make the most impact. Done right, coaching leadership uses an open, caring and truthful approach that comes from the heart.

One of the big benefits of the coaching style is the trust it builds between you and your employees. When leaders adopt a coaching style, they seek to gain clarity on the thoughts, feelings and emotions of their employees. Imagine how Kevin's meeting with Christina could have been different if he used a true coaching style. If he had come from a place of caring, the meeting would have looked very different. Instead of saying to Christina, "I won't tolerate this anymore," Kevin could have said something like, "Christina, you've always been a reliable, committed employee. Lately I've noticed that something

57

has changed. You've missed work days and arrived late to work. I want to be sure I'm supporting you." Do you see the difference between the conversation Kevin had with Christina, and the one he could have had if he had used both his head and his heart? This scenario opens the door for a more open conversation.

Caring + Truth = Compassion

Coaching opens up the channel for compassionate and caring conversations. Unfortunately in today's fast-paced, multi-tasking business environment, managers often don't take the time to have such conversations with their employees. You must learn to balance truth with caring so that you don't come across as blunt or destructive. It's not only what you say to your employees that counts, but the way in which you say it makes the difference. I've witnessed managers resorting to email to deliver difficult news to an employee, rather than having a caring, in-person meeting. Caring + Truth is the equation for all your interactions with your employees, whether in person or, for more routine communications, via email or phone.

I've also had clients who fear telling the truth to their employees, almost as if telling the truth were considered to be mean-spirited. However, without hearing the truth, how will an employee know exactly what behaviors or situations need to be addressed? A client, Josh, recently told me he believed in being "brutally honest" with people, but felt as though it was not an accepted practice in his organization. My question for Josh was, "Is it possible to take the 'brutal' out of your conversations, and just be honest with his employees, though in a caring way?"

Both feedback and coaching are gifts you give to your employees. Without this, your staff can't improve, learn new skills and experience career growth. But, always make sure you're giving feedback and coaching with compassion.

♟

You get the best efforts from others not by lighting a fire beneath them,
but by building a fire within.

—Screenwriter and Academy Award nominee Bob Nelson

Chapter Six

Building Trust

The coaching leader's foundation

While trust is the foundation of all successful relationships, including the relationships between coaching leaders and their employees, it appears to be in short supply. Fallout from years of a challenging business environment has eroded employees' trust in their leaders. The results of a "Building Trust in Business" Survey showed that employees often are distrustful of their leaders, especially in the areas of transparency, managing change, power-sharing through delegation and providing feedback to employees. Low-trust atmospheres are dissatisfying places to work, especially for high-performers who will leave a low-trust company or low-trust boss as the job market improves.

"Multiple studies show that high-trust organizations outperform low trust organizations by up to three times," comments Stephen M. R. Covey, author of <u>Smart Trust:</u> <u>Creating Prosperity, Energy, and Joy in a Low-Trust World.</u> When trust is low, communications, transactions and decisions are slower, due to excess bureaucracy, double-checking, second-guessing, etc. This reduces the speed of conducting business and increases costs. "Smart trust," as

Covey describes it, is that sweet spot between the blind trust of gullibility and the kind of trust that comes from both your heart (an ability to trust) and your head (analyzing the situation). Smart trust, he says, creates an atmosphere of "opportunities and possibilities without taking naive risks in a world where not everyone can be trusted."

So, how do we create a safe environment of mutual respect, one that is the foundation of the culture you want to have in your organization. Trust between two people requires each to have confidence in one another and to feel they can speak openly to each another without fear. Building trust with employees results in a more harmonious, more productive and creative work environment. When there is a healthy relationship based upon trust:

- Communication is open and honest.
- Everyone works together creating solutions to achieve goals.
- There is more innovation and creativity.
- Employees are committed to the company's overall success.
- Employees will create breakthrough results.

Starting a new position with a trust challenge

A new communication manager was hired just as the company became embroiled in a public relations issue. The staff she inherited had been with the company for years, and one of them felt he should have been promoted into the communication management position, rather than bringing in someone from the outside who did not know the company well.

The new manager could have handled the PR issue herself because it did require a quick response. Instead, she took "a leap of faith," seeing the PR problem as an opportunity to build a trusting relationship between her and her staff. She called her staff into a meeting, outlined the situation and asked them to use their knowledge of the company to develop a strategy to address the PR issue. After some hours, the staff had crafted a proposal for the company's response. When the communication manager proposed the plan to the CEO, she brought along the senior staff member who felt he had been passed over for promotion, to give an important part of the presentation. The manager recognized all members of the staff for working together to develop an appropriate, effective and timely response to the PR problem.

How do you think her staff viewed the new manager's approach? Did she build trust? Did she show appreciation for their unique talents? Did she start building a trusting relationship with the staff member who felt passed over?

Despite the challenges of starting a new position and immediately confronting a PR crisis, along with a staff that was wary or even hostile to her, the new manager took steps to build trust with her employees. She called on her new staff to use their unique talents in helping to

63

address the PR issue and recognized them for their contributions. She also showcased the ability of the staff member who felt he should have received the promotion. No doubt you'd agree that the new manager was off to a very positive start.

THE TRUST LENS

To build trust we need to better understand how it is created. Each of us has a subconscious "trust lens" that processes the way we think about another person. Your trust lens has two sides: the right side is how you see yourself, and the left side is how you see the other person. Your trust lens ultimately impacts the actions you take toward another person. Below is a simple diagram of your trust lens.

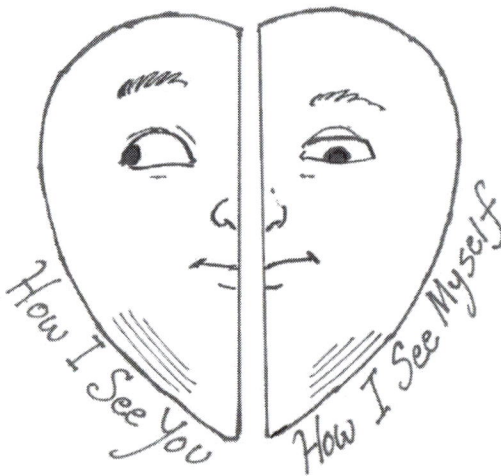

Why is your trust lens shown as a heart? We all remember

the story of "The Wizard of Oz," where the fearful lion is on a journey to the wizard to get a heart—the symbol of courage. Building trust requires us to be courageous enough to open ourselves to others in an honest and unpretentious way, not so that people can take advantage of us but so people know we care about them as individuals. It also takes courage for us to have self-awareness—to understand who we are and how we interact with others so we can strengthen our ability to engage and motivate others.

Without both sides, your trust lens subconsciously selects and interprets information based upon your core beliefs and internal set of rules, and collects evidence "confirming" that your reality is correct. It takes courage—and heart—to let go of both past experiences and misinterpretations that may interfere with building trust. At the same time, employees need to feel valued, respected and cared about through the eyes of you, the manager, before they can see their own true intelligence, worth and value. That doesn't mean you're a "push over." You can still have high expectations for performance and hold people accountable, but you do need to approach employees from a positive, not negative, view.

The only way you can build trust with an employee is to understand how your trust lens works and how it may be interfering with the situation or issue. You need to "suspend" your trust lens for a time so you can listen without pre-judgment and know where the employee is coming from.

Much like a beating heart, your trust lens is continually processing thoughts and feelings. Let's imagine your trust lens at work. Can you think of a relationship—perhaps with an employee—in which the level of trust is less than ideal? With that relationship in mind, work through the questions below. Generally, the first answer that pops into your head is the right one.

Beginning at the right side of your trust lens...

How I See Myself

1. What do I think about myself in this relationship?

   - [ ] Am I partnering with the employee to create positive results?

   - [ ] Do I bring out the best in this employee?

   - [ ] Am I open-minded or closed-minded?

   - [ ] Do I communicate openly or do I withhold information?

2. How do I feel about myself in this relationship?

   - [ ] Am I confident (or insecure) about my abilities and skills to succeed as a leader?

   - [ ] Do I feel proud that I'm honest, or do I feel disappointed because I sometimes stretch the truth?

☐ Am I motivated to do the right things to support the employee's success?

☐ Do I feel comfortable sharing my feelings with the employee?

3. What <u>actions</u> do I typically take in this relationship?

Do I keep my commitments?

Do I treat the employee respectfully?

Is my behavior consistent?

Do I create clarity around expected results?

Moving to the left side of the trust lens...

How I See You

4. What do I <u>think</u> about the employee?

Is the employee partnering with me to create positive results?

Does the employee try to bring out the best in me?

Is the employee open-minded (or closed-minded)?

Does the employee communicate openly (or does he or she withhold information)?

5. How do I <u>feel</u> about the employee?

keep reading all prints that follow.

Am I confident (or insecure) about the employee's ability and skills to succeed in his or her role?

Do I feel good that the employee is honest (or do I feel disappointed because he or she sometimes stretches the truth)?

Am I positive that the employee is motivated to do the right things to support the company's success?

Am I satisfied that the employee is comfortable sharing their feelings?

6. What are my perceptions of <u>the employee's actions</u>?

Do I believe the employee keeps commitments?

Do I think the employee treats me respectfully?

Do I trust that the employee's behavior is consistent?

Do I think the employee is clear about expected results?

Do you believe that your relationship with your employee is affected by what you see in yourself? Would seeing something different about your employee change your relationship? The way you feel about yourself and the way you feel about the other person determines your reality, which can either build or hinder the amount of trust between the two of you. For instance, if you see the employee as someone who does just enough to collect a paycheck, you will view anything that employee does or the discussion you have with that employee through that lens. You need to let go of that view and regard the employee with objectivity and respect.

BUILDING TRUST

One of the biggest jobs for any leader is to inspire trust. But to inspire trust as a leader, you must step up and go first, trusting in others. If you don't trust others, they will not trust you. Look back at the questions above and find the questions that might help you identify your biggest challenge in building trust. If your employees believe that you have their best interests at heart, then they will consider you to be operating with integrity. This in turn will open the door for a more trusting relationship. Likewise, seeing the best in the employee will transform your actions towards that person. The net result will be increased trust and a better relationship.

When Trust Was Wearing Thin

There were only three days left until the end of the month and Jeff hadn't yet met his sales goal. Teresa, his manager, noticed that Jeff was spending too much time at the desk instead of being out in the field. Her gut said there must be a problem. In the past, Teresa would have chided Jeff for not getting out of the office and drumming up business. (Not exactly the way to inspire trust.) But Teresa had committed to adopting a new style of leadership during our coaching work together. She was making every effort to be conscious of being truthful, but caring, and inspiring trust in her employees.

Theresa decided to have a coaching session with Jeff and approached the session with the belief that Jeff truly wanted to meet his sales goal. During their conversation, Teresa discovered that Jeff was having trouble closing a deal with a large client. He didn't know what else to do and was very discouraged. Teresa acknowledged Jeff by reminding him that the reason he was so successful is that he always had his clients' best interests at heart. Teresa and Jeff brainstormed possible solutions for reaching his goals with this particular client.

As a coaching leader, Teresa demonstrated that she cared about Jeff in his efforts to achieve his goals. Jeff soon recognized Teresa's newfound level of care and support; he quickly "loosened up," resulting in a solutions-focused conversation. With his renewed energy and a dash of enthusiasm ignited by the sense that his manager trusted him and his talent, he set out to close another big sale. It all started with Teresa having confidence in herself and then trusting Jeff's skills and abilities. Jeff's renewed passion and determination made all the difference in producing the successful outcome – an excellent result from Theresa's coaching session!

REBUILDING BROKEN TRUST

Most of us have been on both sides of broken trust, and the most difficult place to be is the person who initiated the wrongful situation. Turning the situation around is even more difficult.

Making it right again

Gail, a former client of mine, felt betrayed by her manager when he made her the scapegoat of a decision he authorized. Gail and her team had developed a new Customer Service IT system, and successfully tested it within a smaller company division. Given that it had performed flawlessly in that division, Gail asked her manager if he thought the new IT system was ready to go "live" companywide. He agreed. Unfortunately, because of some previously unknown software differences in a few other divisions, the new system crashed. When the IT vice president came storming into the manager's office and demanded to know who implemented the new software system, the startled manager blurted out that Gail and her team had done this work.

While technically true, it was the manager who had approved the implementation. When Gail heard about what her manager had said, she felt that she and her staff been "thrown under the bus." Trust between Gail and her manager had been broken.

After a period of angst and regret, the manager approached Gail with an apology. He committed to making amends and changing the outcome. In Gail's presence, he called the vice president and said that, although Gail and her team had implemented the system after careful "beta" testing, it was he who had authorized the system to go live companywide. After he hung up the phone, the manager told Gail that from now on, he would be sure to take the consequences of go-ahead decisions he had made. And he worked directly with Gail and the team to rectify the software problem.

Truthfully, it can take a lot of time and effort to build trust again. It will take icebreaking courage to come together to acknowledge how you feel and to really listen to the other person. Additionally, it will require a mutual commitment to move forward in a productive and healthy way by letting go of the past and making plans to handle things differently in the future.

Here are some suggestions on how to rebuild trust:

- Acknowledge your own mistakes.
- Talk about what trust means to each of you, as trust might mean different things to different people.
- Take small sincere actions that demonstrate you can be trusted.
- Describe your commitment to rebuild trust, as it is the foundation to this relationship.
- Continue to "walk your talk."

Some people come to a relationship with an inherent lack of trust: They may have an expectation of how they will be treated based on previous experiences. As you change your behavior, others may question your sincerity at first. Hang in there. Ensure that your actions match your words.

The goal is not only to change the way in which you have conversations with your employees, but also to approach those conversations with compassion and with an intention to improve the relationship.

Here is where the trust lens comes back into play. Take another look at your lens and examine again what you believe to be true. Can you see the positive intentions in the employee? Can you commit to thoughts and actions that will rebuild this trusting relationship?

The only way we can rebuild trust again is to give trust away and believe that the employee will return that trust to you. This is hard but rewarding work if you are willing to trust the other person in your quest to regain a healthy relationship.

♟

Self-trust is the first secret of success.

—American Poet Ralph Waldo Emerson

♟

Trust men and they will be true to you.
Treat them greatly, and they will show themselves great.

—American Poet Ralph Waldo Emerson

Chapter Seven

Become a Great Listener

Listen to understand, rather than to reply

Are you a good listener? Most of us probably consider ourselves to be pretty good listeners, so I suspect your reply to that question is affirmative. If your answer to that question is *no*, you're more self-aware than the rest of us.

Learning to say NO to distractions means choosing to say YES to your employees.

Before delving into this chapter, I encourage you to take this three-minute *Listening Skills Assessment.* It will help you determine how much you really focus—amid all the distractions—on listening to your employees and fully understanding what they really are saying.

LISTENING SKILLS ASSESSMENT

Answer these 10 questions based on the scale below to gauge your listening skills. (Scale: 4 - Almost Always; 3 - Usually; 2 - Seldom; 1 - Never)

1. I make effective eye contact throughout the conversation to let the person know that I am listening.	
2. I am patient to wait until the other person has stopped speaking before I speak.	
3. I summarize, restate or paraphrase in my own words what I believe the other person is saying to make sure that I have it right.	
4. I ask clarifying questions to more fully understand the other person's ideas or intentions.	
5. I withhold judgment or criticism of the other person's positions or points of view.	
6. I listen fully even though I think I know what the other person is about to say.	
7. I notice what the other person is *not* saying and I inquire about it so that I can fully understand.	
8. I stop what I am doing and minimize distractions by giving full attention to the other person.	
9. I remember and recall the details of the other person's ideas or important points made during the conversation.	

10. I pay close attention to non-verbal messages from the other person when they are speaking.	
Your Total Score	

If you scored 40, congratulations! You are a very good listener. The majority of the people who have taken this quiz have scored less than 40. Take a few minutes and write the top 3 listening skills that you believe will best improve your interactions and overall results with others.

1._____

2._____

3._____

Even if you are an outstanding listener, I encourage you to read on, as there may be a few tips that will help you become an even better listener. If your score was below outstanding, you are not alone and you'll also find helpful pointers in this chapter.

MOST MANAGERS BELIEVE THEY LISTEN

When is the last time you dropped what you were doing to truly listen to one of your employees? By "truly listening," I mean closing your office door to block out all noise and distractions; clearing your mind of everything except for that employee, with your focus 100 percent on him or her. In today's multi-tasking business world, it's undoubtedly rare for you to listen to an employee without interruptions. You may be listening while you're going through paperwork, or you may be listening while thinking about the conversation you just had with a vendor. You might be listening to your employee and trying to solve a problem while they're speaking.

My observation is that true listening doesn't come naturally for most of us. As a manager, you need to get the job done. As such, you're likely focused on what your employees say about what they've accomplished, how they spent their time and how to solve their problems. The charge of a manager is to direct others, so most of the time; our instinct is to tell someone what to do, rather than to listen. We have difficulty stopping ourselves from saying what we know, what we think, and telling our employees what they should do next.

Not what you want to hear

Ron got a call on his cell phone just as he walked back into his office from a meeting that challenged his patience and coping skills to the max. On the other end of the phone was his employee, Emily, telling him that the report she had promised was not going to be in on time, but would get it to him next week. Ron responded, "Get it to me by the end of the day tomorrow or we are going to be in big trouble." In this case, he only heard her one sentence, but that was all that he needed to blast out a command. Was there more to the story that he should have heard? Was something going on with his customers that might have caused the report to be delayed? Was Emily having a personal emergency that was preventing her from meeting the report deadline? Before he took the time to listen to Emily and ask some probing questions, he had already created a negative experience with Emily that he would later have to correct. And he might have forced her to write a report that had incomplete information and could have angered customers and his superiors.

This example shows that listening skills are key to our success as managers and coaching leaders—not to mention winning the talent war. A few more conversations like this and Emily might decide her talents would be more appreciated at another company.

HOW WE LEARNED TO LISTEN

In all likelihood, we learned listening skills from our parents. In my house, everyone got his or her "turn" to speak. Many of us still follow that guideline today: You take your turn and I'm next. Chances are that while you're taking your turn, the next person is thinking about what he or she is going to say. It's natural for us because we want to be prepared to answer--a lesson we probably learned in school. However, as we consider our next comment, we stop listening because our brains are engaged in the thinking process. We want to sound brilliant when it's our turn to speak, so we think we must stop listening to focus on what we want to say next. Or do we?

The antidote to this type of back-and-forth is *curiosity.* To engage in being curious, you must fully focus on what the other person is saying. You must be "in the moment." We've all heard the adage, "Curiosity killed the cat." But actually, curiosity is what helps the cat understand its surroundings, be alert to danger and detect that tiny mouse hiding in your basement. When you listen with curiosity, there is no judgment, no need to agree or disagree. You are simply paying attention—with great interest.

Leaders who truly listen to their employees do so with

curiosity. They want to know what the person is really saying. Once the employee has finished speaking, the leader takes time to think first and then respond. This is an important point and bears repeating: In today's 24/7 world of television, cell phones, the Internet, Facebook and Twitter, we usually experience rapid-fire conversations with little time for thought between one-liners. However, in the real world, we can take a few seconds to consider what we've just heard from an employee (or anyone else, for that matter) before responding. Listen fully and intently, think carefully about what you've heard, and reflect what you've come to understand in your comment. Then, your employee will know he or she was understood and you will not miss important information.

THE VALUE OF LISTENING

In your journey from manager to coaching leader, one of the key skills you must master is that of genuine listening that seeks to understand those with whom you work. It's not until you listen *and understand*—not only to what they are saying, but also to discover what they may be thinking, and feeling—that you can discern how to best respond and support your employees.

As a leader, we feel we must be "smart." We must have all of the answers. When an employee comes to us for support, our natural tendency is to solve the problem or give an opinion. In my survey, 75 percent of the business leaders who responded said that when an employee comes to them with a problem, they typically tell that employee what to do. In today's business environment, where instant action is expected, it's a challenge for a leader to be quiet and listen, to probe for reasons behind the problem or help the employee figure out the solution on his or her own.

However, it's only when we truly listen that we learn who others are, and what is on their minds and in their hearts. My belief is that listening makes the biggest difference in obtaining positive outcomes from any communication. In Stephen Covey's best-selling book, *The Seven Habits of Highly Effective People,* the fifth habit is *seek first to understand and then to be understood*. Notice that he put "to understand" (to listen) *before* "to be understood" (to be heard). It's an important distinction. To understand, we must first listen - to truly listen at a *deep* level.

Your employees *want and need* to be understood by you. When individuals are understood, they feel affirmed and validated. When your employees feel acknowledged by you (through your listening to them), they will more willingly align with your direction and company goals.

Think back to our story of Kevin and Christina in Chapter Five. Kevin never took the time to understand. He never asked Christina what happened that caused her to be late so often and why she'd called in sick so many times in the past month. By listening to your employees and their needs, the solutions are more likely to match what they really need. Often, managers solve the problem for their employees (or at least believe they are solving a problem), but they don't really have all the information. Thus, managers can go down the wrong path for solutions. By listening to understand, managers are able to more fully comprehend the problem and help employees develop their own solutions. The result is often better because employees may have insights that result in a better solution and they feel ownership of the action plan they developed mutually with their manager.

TWO TYPES OF LISTENING

Listening at a deep level isn't easy. Though there are many different types of listening, I have simplified them into two major types: everyday listening and exceptional listening.

EVERYDAY LISTENING

The first type of listening is the kind most of us do all the time. In everyday listening, we "sort of" listen: we hear the words, but our minds are elsewhere, on other people, things or problems. We listen to the other person's words, while trying to figure out what impact it may have on us, or what we would do in this situation. We're more focused on ourselves than on the individual who is speaking: we're more focused on our own thoughts, our judgments on the topic and how it makes us feel.

This type of listening occurs in all kinds of conversations: in families, with friends, at work, and... between you and your employees. Have you ever been in one of the following situations?

> You're in conversation with someone and the other person is talking. You're listening (or so you think.) You're even nodding as if completely engaged in the conversation. Then the other person asks you a question. You're caught off-guard and realize you missed an important point. If this happens in a meeting with customers or in a conversation with your boss, you risk losing a sale or offending your own manager.

> Someone is telling you about an incident at work. It

sounds like something you've heard often before, so you listen to only select portions of what the person is saying. You may even "hear" something that wasn't said because you thought you knew where the narrative was going. As a result, you heard what you *expected* the other person to say, not what he really said. What if the incident had a different ending than you expected? What if it was something you needed to know about and act on?

While everyday listening is what we're accustomed to, as coaching leaders we must embrace a higher level of listening.

EXCEPTIONAL LISTENING

With exceptional listening, you must be in the moment, fully focused on the other person with the commitment and intention to gain a complete understanding. Be sure to prepare yourself and your environment for this type of listening: Clear your desk and turn off all unnecessary electronics. Better yet, have the conversation where you're assured of no distractions. Find a time for the conversation that is right for you, and allows you to let go (for a few minutes) of what is on your desk and on your mind.

Exceptional listening requires a 100 percent focus and commitment to comprehend. It involves not only hearing the words, but also observing body language, and even listening for indications of the individual's thoughts, feelings and emotions, such as tone of voice and facial expressions. You then communicate your understanding with appropriate body language, facial expressions and nods. When you utilize exceptional listening with your employees, you demonstrate your confidence in them; you confirm that you value them; you convey that they are important and what they have to say is significant. Peter Senge, director of the Center for Organizational Learning, says this about listening: "To listen fully means to pay close attention to what is being said beneath the words. You listen not only to the 'music,' but to the essence of the person speaking."

As coaching leaders hone their listening skills, they begin to listen for more than just the words. They listen not only with their ears, but also with their eyes and hearts. They listen for energy and emotion and for what's *not* being said. They listen with curiosity and without judgment. They don't try to figure anything out. This is the most ideal form, the highest form, of listening.

It's also a vital part of winning the talent war—attracting, motivating and retaining the best people. Employees who feel that their manager listens to them and cares about their career growth are more likely to stay with an organization.

Now that you've grasped the importance of exceptional listening, let's move on to Chapter Eight, which is about how to ask the right questions that lead to the best solutions for you and your employees.

♟

One of the best ways to persuade others is with your ears—

by listening to them.

—Aviator and Entrepreneur Dean Rush

Ask Questions To Uncover Solutions

Your employees have the answers;

they just might not know it

When adopting a coaching style, listening is the primary skill for a leader to master. Once we listen, what's next? *Questioning* is listening's ":significant other." The art of questioning helps your employees to learn, discover and grow. Good questions draw out the best in your employees; questioning helps them to think and take responsibility for results. In addition, when you truly listen to their answers, you will better understand. Listening and asking questions go hand-in-hand. To be able to ask powerful questions, you must first listen with focused attention.

The reason why leaders have trouble with relying on questioning is because we don't always have the answer. And of course, it is not always the best choice to make assumptions about what the answers are for your employees. Sometimes the assumptions that we are making aren't even close to their reality.

Don't Judge a Person by her Accent

We all have things that label us. It might be our height, a mannerism, hair color, the way we dress or many other things. *For me, it's my Texas accent.*

There were times the sound of my voice defined me before anyone listened to the words I spoke. The feeling of inferiority due to my accent stayed with me for years. For example, in a prospective job interview, an executive recruiter in Boston dismissed me as soon as he heard me speak, saying that I didn't sound smart enough.

Later I decided to ask people what they thought about my accent. I was in for a surprise; most people expressed a positive reaction to my accent. I was told that it creates a sense of gentility, openness, and kindness. People may still judge me based on my accent, but the judgments tend to be more positive than negative.

Are your assumptions true? One way to deal with a preconception is to get curious, question it and ask others. We need to question our assumptions about our employees, without always being so quick in making decisions. It might be good to allow the answers to unfold naturally. Take the time to be willing to hear your employee's answer even if it is not what you are expecting. In those moments, it's helpful to stay open to the fact that reality could be something different than you had originally thought and may lead to a better solution. It's a good habit to challenge your beliefs and allow for more creative solutions.

QUESTIONING HELPS YOU FIND YOUR SWEET SPOT

It will take courage to push through the unknown to ask others for their thoughts and ideas. And, for you to find your sweet spot as a leader, you must ask good questions to find out more about who your employees are and what they need to be successful – to help you be successful too! When you are committed to helping your employees get what they need, you are having a positive impact. Through questioning you will involve your employees in creating solutions and, very importantly, in shaping their own *careers*.

Asking your employees great questions...

- **Engages** them to expand their own awareness.
- **Supports** them in taking ownership for their personal growth, development, and progress.
- **Honors** them for who they are and what they do.
- **Demonstrates** your interest in what they have to say.
- **Establishes** trust and rapport.
- **Builds** a relationship of mutual respect.

Questioning allows your employees to be personally responsible not only for figuring out their desired future within your organization, but also for discovering what they must do to achieve that future. Of course, it's not just about the future; much of your conversations with employees will be about now. If you are focused on your employees, you will need to ask questions that support them in achieving their current responsibilities and goals. Asking good questions is a great leadership technique and an important part of coaching leadership.

ASKING THE RIGHT QUESTIONS

There are two major types of questions: open-ended and closed-ended. A question that can be answered very simply, with either a yes or no, or with a limited response of a few words, is a closed-ended question. Most managers are accustomed to asking closed-ended questions:

Did you finish your report?
Have you talked with your customer yet?
Were your numbers on target for last week?

Closed-ended questions do not give you, the leader, an opportunity to engage in a real conversation that allows you to draw out more information or perspectives from your employees. When you adopt a coaching style, focus on minimizing your closed-ended questions and maximizing your open-ended questions.

Open-ended questions are designed to elicit thoughtful responses and encourage meaningful dialogue. They make room for more than simple answers, numbers and details: they allow you to discover "what's up, what matters, what if, what else and what's next." These types of questions

typically begin with *what, when,* or *how.* Open-ended
questions may also be in the form of a statement, "Tell me
about..." which encourages a conversation. With a bit of
practice, you will learn the art of asking great open-ended
questions. Here are a few examples:

> *What is happening now?*
> *How is your situation impacting you?*
> *What do you want to see going forward?*
> *How are others responding to your situation?*
> *What will be the payoff when you are successful?*

In a coaching conversation, questioning begins with a
broad perspective and then moves deeper into details.
Once you've captured the big picture, then you can probe
for bits of information that might have been missed, or
something you believe your employee might not have
considered. This helps employees to generate their own
awareness by having the opportunity to verbalize the
situation, and to *hear* what they are actually thinking and
feeling.

QUESTIONS TO AVOID

Leading questions – Questioning is not a trick to influence
your employees to do what you want them to do. Leading
questions suggest a particular answer. (For example,
"Don't you think it would be a good idea to....?") Your
employees are smart and will immediately see that you're
attempting to manipulate them into the "right" answer.
Asking leading questions is a sure-fire way to lose your

employees' trust, instead of building a trusting relationship. You can, however, make a suggestion such as, "Would you mind if I throw out another thought to explore?" This type of question can lead to a brainstorming session between you and your employee.

"Why" questions – More often than not, "why questions" put employees on the defensive. Asking why implies there's something wrong, and makes the other person feel insecure. When you ask your employee "why," you're inferring they've made a mistake, or did something you (as the boss) are now second-guessing. Instead, begin your discovery process with "Tell me about..." or "Help me understand." These types of questions are positive and invite your employee to explore.

Run-on questions – If you've ever gone to a meeting—one in which your colleague was unable to attend—perhaps you were barraged with run-on questions: *What happened to you, who opened the can of worms, oh my....and how did John (the boss) handle things? Wow, what else was said, and what do you think about that?* We've all been on the receiving end of run-on questions and our first reaction is *whoa, slow down!* Don't ask several questions at once. Simply ask one question at a time.

Questions projecting *your* feelings – Steer clear of inserting your feelings and emotions into the questions you ask. For example, "I know that's really sad for you to have had that situation happen; tell me how you feel." In this situation, you would be projecting your own feeling of sadness into the situation when, in fact, the "thing" that happened may be a positive outcome for your employee. Rather, create questions that are expansive—questions that get your employee to think and dig deep. A simpler, yet effective question, would be, "How does that make you feel?"

COME FROM A PLACE OF CURIOSITY

When I was learning how to ask powerful open-ended questions, one tip I found most helpful was to come from a place of curiosity. Putting on the "curiosity hat" makes open-ended questioning much easier. It means being *interested* in what's going on for your employee *without* being judgmental: *What do you think? What's your approach? What's important to you? What's your solution?* When you question from a place of curiosity, you will help your employees to do their own personal discovery.

Some of you may remember the television show Columbo staring Peter Falk. He was a curious homicide detective with the LAPD. Using an inquisitive style he started a conversation, meant to put people at ease, with an "I wonder...." statement, followed by a powerful question. Perhaps this metaphor will help you remember to use the "I wonder" perspective, asking questions driven from curiosity and not judgment.

Coming from a place of curiosity gives you permission to stop trying to "fix" your employee or the situation. (Doesn't it feel good to know that you no longer have to be the one to fix everything?) Trust that your employees will have their own ideas and answers. You are there to help them discover what those might be. Simply be on the side of your employees, championing and encouraging them to be their best, while you are being curious *for them* to draw out their thoughts, feelings and solutions.

POWERFUL QUESTIONS

The best questions are powerful. They are designed to dig deep and get under the surface. Powerful questions are designed to discover more about...

- Thoughts and observations
- Feelings
- What really matters

Below are some examples of powerful questions:

What is your dream goal with this situation?

How would you feel if you accomplished this?

What is important to you about having this outcome?

What have you done in the past that is similar to this situation?

If you were having a conversation with a wise sage, what would he/she tell you?

What else (used to evoke more ideas or potential solutions)?

How will your career be different if you make this happen?

What might be possible if you looked at this from another perspective?

What are you willing to do to produce this result?

What strengths do you have that you could use to make this happen?

Questioning is designed to expand the employee's awareness, not to prove how smart you are or how wrong your employees are. Asking the right questions in the right way ensures clarity, sets proper expectations and builds trust. It helps employees see beyond their current situation to see what's possible.

Listening and asking powerful questions are two of the main "ingredients" that go into the secret sauce of coaching leadership, and getting you into your sweet spot as a leader. When combined with leading from your heart, these new skills will help you create strong relationships of trust with your employees. As your employees become more connected to you and engaged with their positions, I'm confident that you'll see amazing results with your employees and in all aspects of the business, including the bottom line.

Questioning Exercise:

Below are seven poorly structured questions that can lead to defensive or limited responses. Please rewrite the question so that it invites an open discussion.

1. Did you finish the performance reviews?

   _____

   _____

2. Have you scheduled all the appointments?

   _____

   _____

3. Did you meet your sales projections for last month?

   _____

   _____

4. I've been working on this idea for weeks. What do you think of it?

   _____

   _____

5. Why have you been cutting back on attending sales meetings?

    _____

    _____

6. Why has your department racked up a 50% increase in turnover this past year?

    _____

    _____

7. That must have been a hectic day. I would have fallen apart. Why didn't you?

    _____

    _____

With a culture of trust, exceptional listening and asking powerful, open-ended questions, you and your team will be well on your way to achieving your goals and winning the talent war. Now that we've covered how to ask questions that lead to solutions, it's time to move on to how to prepare for and have a coaching conversation.

♟

Ask questions from your heart
and you will be answered from the heart.

— Omaha Proverb

Chapter Nine

I think you can sell this in government. ie. G & A

Coaching Conversations for Breakthrough Results

The STAR coaching model

Armed with listening and questioning skills, you are now ready to learn about the *coaching conversation.* Coaching can happen in any conversation, but typically the coaching style is reserved for a more formal meeting with an employee. Coaching conversations go above and beyond the typical task-oriented conversations, although they could include some performance goals or other issues you and the employee may want to discuss. These conversations are generally focused on the future and what is important for the employee to work towards to help them build their career. Coaching conversations are designed to be a safe place for employees to brainstorm possible solutions to issues they may be facing. Coaching conversations typically include:

- Presenting concerns or opportunities
- Personal performance strategies
- Talent and skill development
- Career advancement

Note: you will not use the coaching style in every conversation with an employee. For example, when providing feedback, a directive style may be more appropriate. In a management meeting, you might use a visionary style to discuss the future of the business.

In coaching conversations, you are not telling your employees what to do; rather, you are assisting your employees in developing their own answers. Your role is to facilitate conversations, engage your employees in various processes of information-gathering and brainstorming, and help them come up with their own solutions. Let's take a look at a four-step process for a coaching conversation - the *STAR coaching model*. Just as generals have stars, so do managers and emerging leaders who aim to win the talent war through the coaching style of leadership.

S STAGE THE MEETING

There are just a few important elements to ensure your meeting gets off to a good start. Before your employee walks in the door, be sure to:

1. Prepare yourself emotionally
2. Create a conducive meeting environment

When you and your employee are both seated and ready to get started, begin the conversation by connecting with your employee.

Prepare yourself – As the leader, it's important to prepare yourself for the coaching conversation. A few minutes before your scheduled meeting, stop whatever else you're working on and *let it go*. I promise you, it will be waiting for you when the meeting is over. Next, ask yourself a couple of questions: *Am I mentally available to have this conversation? And, is there anything that will prevent me from being truly present for this employee?* If you happen to be upset about something, you may not have the right mindset for a coaching conversation. If you feel there's a potential for your focus to be taken away from the conversation—because you have other things on your mind—then take a few minutes in advance to prepare yourself mentally:

- Take a few deep breaths to help clear your mind.
- Reflect on the individual with whom you'll be having the conversation: let go of all

judgments, and note to yourself their positive attributes and contributions to your company.
- Switch your mindset from *"How can this employee help me?"* to *"How can I be helpful to this employee to create a positive outcome for all concerned?"*
- Come to the conversation with a curiosity about what you might learn from your employee that you hadn't realized before.

Prepare the environment – Ensure there are no distractions that might hinder or interrupt a rich conversation:

- Turn off your cell phone
- Turn off your computer monitor
- Close the door once the employee has entered the room, or choose a space for a private and confidential conversation.
- Focus on the topic and outcome – Once your employee is comfortably seated, spend a few moments connecting, building rapport and acknowledge the importance of this time together. Working with the employee at a high level, find the focus for the discussion and identify what outcomes they'd like to take away as a result of the meeting. Consider the following questions as examples:
  - o What would you like to focus on today?

101

- o What's the most important thing for us to talk about?
- o What outcome would you like to achieve in our time together?
- o What opportunity might be created by this conversation?

Remember to take notes during the conversation and encourage the employee to do the same. This is important in helping both of you to capture the topic of the conversation, angles to explore, possible solutions, action steps and deadlines.

If an employee chooses a topic for the coaching conversation, he or she is usually more willing to work on problem-solving or solutions concerning that topic. However, there are times when a manager may want to select a topic and get the employee's ideas on how this could result in an important growth opportunity for the employee.

These questions help to set the stage both for you and for your employee. You both will gain a specific sense of what is important to be discussed along with your employee's desired outcome from your meeting. Lastly, if applicable, confirm the amount of time you have for the conversation.

T TELL THE STORY

I like to begin a coaching conversation by asking, "On a scale of 1–10, with 10 being the best, how are things going for you right now?" This allows the employee to discuss their outlook or current perspective, and gives you the advantage of knowing where they're coming from. Remember to utilize your listening and questioning skills.

Once the stage is set, you now open the floor for your employee to "tell their story," which simply means you allow the employee to discuss their concerns, issues and/or future goals.

The important goal here is to let your employee talk about their point of view. This is your chance to get curious and discover more information by really listening for what specifically is happening in the situation. Remember to utilize your listening and questioning skills. The goal in this step is to find out more about what your employee thinks and feels about the topic and not to be worrying about your own interpretation of the event. How they are reacting and interpreting the event will give you great insight into what questions you can ask that will uncover any gaps and expand their possibilities.

Not only do you want to find out the details of your employee's story but you also want to find out what the situation means to them. It's important to understand what impact they believe this scenario will have on them, and how this will influence their long-term goals. This is the time to hear their perspective, to draw out as much information to find out where expansion is possible. The more you uncover now the richer the next step will be. This open discussion will allow them to see where there might be opportunities to explore new perspectives and create new angles in seeing things going forward.

A ANGLE FOR EXPLORING POSSIBILITIES

In just a few moments, you've received some excellent information: the major concern or challenge the employee has right now. Now it's time to expand the *angle* from which we view the issue, and move to what I call the "discovery process," or exploring ways to create solutions. During this phase of the coaching conversation, you have an opportunity to utilize your questioning skills. Below are some good sample questions to ask employees that will help facilitate their discovery process:

Determine the results your employee wants:

- What would success look like in this situation?
- Exactly what is it that you want to happen?

Learn from past experiences:

- Tell me about a time when you were able to do this before.
- What have you accomplished already?
- What worked and what didn't work as well as you had hoped?
- What lessons from your past could help you in this situation?

Explore new perspectives:

- What strengths and skills do you have that will help you?
- How can you learn additional necessary skills?
- What could be a different approach than you have tried before?
- What other resources are available to you?
- What would be a positive perspective on this situation?
- What thoughts and actions could you change in order to try something new?
- What new ideas do you have about getting where you want to go?
- I don't have one "right" answer, but let's brainstorm together about what's possible for you.

The key is to ask powerful questions to get your employees to come up with possible solutions so they can achieve their desired outcomes.

R REACH TO THE FUTURE

The last step in the coaching conversation is all about how to move forward, with you and your employee making the commitment to do so. Here are some questions to ask employees to help them reach to the future and get into action:

- What goals would you like to establish and by when?
- How will you prioritize your actions?
- What first steps will you take?
- How will you know when you've achieved those goals?
- What support do you need from me?
- What else might be helpful?
- How will others know about the changes you are making?
- What additional commitments are you willing to make?

Once your discovery process has concluded, recap the commitments your employee has made, making sure that there is a mutual understanding of important action steps, deadlines and desired outcomes, along with how you can support your employee going forward. To conclude the meeting, ask your employee how the discussion went, if it was helpful, what worked and what was a challenge during the meeting. Finally, set and confirm the time of your next meeting.

For some of you, the "coaching conversation" will be a departure from the management style you've used in the past. Don't worry if you don't get it "just right" the first time. You'll have plenty of opportunities to practice your new skills with your employees as time goes on. In fact, both you and your employees will get better at it. As employees recognize the new leadership approach you are taking, they'll come to coaching conversations better prepared each time. Simply remember to keep the "big three" skills in mind for all your new interactions with employees: Good listening skills, asking powerful questions, and a big dose of leading with your heart in each person-to-person connection.

There is light at the end of the tunnel.

EXAMPLE OF A COACHING CONVERSATION

In this scenario, the manager has already taken the time to prepare for the meeting.

Stage the meeting

Manager: It's been a busy week at work. How are things going for you?

Employee: It sure has been pretty wild for me. I've been working a lot of overtime with Dave's group.

Manager: So for our time today, what would you like to focus on?

Employee: I'd like to get some guidance from you about something that's going on.

Manager: Okay, tell me more about what you'd like to discuss.

Employee: I have been spending a lot of time working with Dave on the new product rollout. My concern is that I am not sure what part of these responsibilities I should be taking on and what part doesn't belong to me.

Manager: We've got 45 minutes to talk. What would you like to accomplish in in the time we have today?

Employee: I need to know how to handle these extra requests. Dave is a real dynamo and has a way of getting people to do way more than they expected. I know I'm responsible for helping pull this project together but I want to know how far I should go in performing extra work. I want a strategy for how to handle Dave and any such requests more effectively next time.

Manager: So the outcome is that you would like to know how to handle Dave and others who may ask you for extra work going forward, right?

Employee: Exactly.

IX- **Tell the Story**

Manager: Let's begin with you telling me more details about what happened this week with Dave.

Employee: This past week, I've spent 20 hours working on the rollout project, doing a lot of tasks on a special request from Dave. At first I didn't mind—that is until I realized how little had been done to gather the market analysis.

Manager: Wow, that involved a lot of work. How did you feel about that?

Employee: Yes, it was a lot of work. I really felt frustrated. This project deserves a good job to make it successful. But Dave and his group should have done more preparatory work before I took on the project management assignment. I had plenty of other work on my plate

Manager: Now that you've done the extra work on Dave's project, what are the implications for you downstream?

Employee: I like working with Dave and his group but I need to set some boundaries about what work I should be doing and not doing. This is an important project for the company's future, and I want it to go well. But I have other projects that deserve my full attention.

Manager: So longer-term, how could you benefit by setting boundaries on what you should not be doing?

Employee: I'd be more effective at what I do if I could better plan for these extra requests. I'd also like to do a better job of setting expectations.

Manager: Are there any other benefits to addressing this issue?

Employee: At the end of the day, I'm likely to be more proactive rather than reactive .

Angle to Explore

Manager: In a best case scenario, how would you like to deal with Dave and his team?

Employee: I want to be able to address a request for support that comes my way, balance my current work and still provide the assistance my internal clients need.

Manager: So let's do some brainstorming about ways to manage these requests. Have you ever had a situation in the past where you got a request for extra work and it went smoothly?

Employee: At my last company, I knew all the players and their management styles. That's because I worked with them in a different capacity before I went into project management. So people knew me and what I could provide. As a result, we worked together more smoothly.

Manager: Could you apply something about that to this situation?

Employee: I'm really not sure what I did. Because I knew people at my former company better, it was easier for me to dig into the situation and asked more questions.

Manager: What are those questions? Can we jot some down?

Employee: Sure, that is definitely doable.

Manager: Could we test these questions to see if it makes sense to use them at this company?

Employee: Let me give that some thought. I need to sit down, think through this and come up with a good flow.

Manager: Would this same approach—digging into the situation and asking more questions—work with Dave's dynamo style?

Employee: Yes, in that moment when I heard that Dave needed help, it would have been great to have these prepared questions. And, it would have helped to find out more details about what and why things needed to be done, and determine ways to get the information without me doing it personally.

Manager: Are there any other possibilities that we might also brainstorm?

Employee: It would help if I started reaching out and building relationships so I'd be more confident working with new people. However, this might take some time.

Manager: What first steps could you take to get to know people here better?

Employee: I can take the initiative to start meeting people to get to know them better.

111

Reach to the future

Manager: We've talked about some great ideas. What specific goals would you like to set?

Employee: I would like to feel confident that I knew the right questions to ask and to determine roles and responsibility so that everyone is 20/20 with expectations.

Manager: That's awesome, you are really good at obtaining clarity with the workload. I think it's a great idea to be prepared up front. How do you plan to do that?

Employee: I am going to sit down and write out questions that would help me develop more of a consulting approach. And I am going to start setting up meetings with people that I will be working closely with on projects, so I can get to know them and how they work. Then, I will draft a list of all the items that have come up so that we can discuss who should complete them and make sure that nothing is missing. That should cut down on all of the reactionary requests.

Manager: Those sound like very important steps. When would you like to have this done?

Employee: By the end of next week I want to develop the questions and flow for how I would like to structure the conversations. And I'll also prepare a list of people that I'd like to meet.

Manager: Is there anything that could get in the way of accomplishing this?

Employee: No. I am going to block out time to get this done because I see how valuable this is.

Manager: I think this is a great game plan. How can I support you?

Employee: How about I take the first pass and then we can review everything next week?

Manager: Sure. Is this time next Friday good for you? Maybe we can even role-play your questions and conversation flow so we can see how it goes. I could also go over your list of people to meet and see if there are others you may also want to include.

Employee: Yes, next Friday at the same time sounds good. Thanks for your help in talking this through. I think this is just what I needed!

On the next page you will find a convenient template for your next coaching conversation that allows you to take notes as you move through the process.

STAR COACHING MODEL

STAGE	Prepare yourself & the environment	
	Determine the topic of the meeting	
	Determine the outcome for the meeting	
TELL	Tell what is happening	
	Tell what is the reaction	
	Tell what it means	
ANGLE	Determine the desirable results	
	Learn from the past	
	Explore new possibilities	
REACH	Establish goals	
	Agree to specific actions	
	Plan and commitment	

Coaching leads to better communication, more trust, and more connection between you, your employees and the business. That's something to celebrate! And we'll talk about that very thing when you turn the page...

♟

There is no such thing as a worthless conversation,
provided you know what to listen for.
And questions are the breath of life for a conversation.

— Author James Nathan Miller

Chapter Ten

Celebrate Success

Acknowledge your employees

Everyone wants to feel the work they do makes a contribution to the organization that employs them. The results of the Towers Watson study (referenced in the introduction and chapter four) shows that employees will eagerly "step up" and contribute more when they feel valued not only as employees, but also as people. The study observed that the more an employee feels valued and appreciated, the more that employee is willing to contribute. When your employees feel they are working hard and supporting others towards win-win solutions, they believe that they are an important part of the team. It's what I call feeling that you're "in the game." One of the biggest challenges faced by leaders is getting their employees in the game—and keeping them there. Leading with heart will help you to do both. When your employees are in the game, they will produce results, everyone will be happy, and this is what it means to find your sweet spot as a leader.

APPRECIATION

I have a question for you: When was the last time you told an employee you genuinely appreciated them as an individual, and that their contributions made an important difference to you and the company? In other words, when is the last time you communicated with your employee using your heart—and not your head? It's this simple act of *acknowledgement* that makes all the difference. Simply defined, *acknowledgment is to recognize something (or someone) for what it truly is, to appreciate the work that has been done, and to be grateful for the existence of another human being.* Each of us has a basic need for recognition. We want to be recognized for who we are and what we do.

A recent study, the "Workforce Mood Tracker™ The Spring 2012 Report titled <u>The Growing Influence of</u>

Employee Recognition, found that "Appreciation is the fuel that drives not only worker happiness, but also worker motivation. Positive recognition from managers and peers has been proven to make a significant difference in engagement." The survey concluded that recognition equates to motivation and success not only for employees, but also for employers and is key to winning the talent war.

This would be a great time to take a few minutes to think about how and when you verbalize your appreciation for your employees. Showing appreciation should be a lot more than simply offering a few compliments at random times (maybe when your day is going well and you're in a good mood). Rather, it should be something that's done with intent and purpose to create and deliver genuine acknowledgement. Take time to consider—and write down—the benefits of recognizing and appreciating the good work of your employees. Understanding those benefits will help encourage you to make it a regular part of your work calendar. Perhaps your company has a formal process where customers tell you about how your employee made a real difference to them. However, it's just as important to single out a good job whenever and wherever it happens, because not all employees have direct contact with customers.

I'm challenging you to be more conscious of recognizing your employees: catch them doing the right thing and tell them. Appreciate them for the individuals they are and for contributing to the success of your business. People notice you've noticed. Anything you can do to recognize and appreciate your employees contributes to making your business a great place to work—for everyone.

ACKNOWLEDGMENT

Acknowledging employees for work well done is certainly an area where using your heart comes into play. Comments such as "great job," "good work," and "nice report" are good temporary boosts once in a while. However, they fall short of a real opportunity to speak to the qualities and the strengths that employee is demonstrating in order to deliver these accomplishments.

Heart-based acknowledgment is done best when it's personal, positive and focuses on the individual strengths and skills of the person on the receiving end. The order of the conversation is important, too. Speak to those individual skills, talents and strengths before the results are addressed. The goal is to not only notice who this person is, but to continually bring out the best in them on a personal level. When this happens, you are strengthening the relationship and building trust in each other, showing a strong alignment between who the person is, what is happening and what success looks like.

By using acknowledgements, you are providing a great motivator to inspire a person to continue with desirable behaviors. Here are some examples of verbal acknowledgements:

"You are very thoughtful and kind, and it shows in the way you build relationships with our customers."

"You are such a good communicator; you can always share your thoughts with others in a convincing way that bring your ideas to life."

"You have such strength of focus; you have the ability to keep yourself and everyone on target."

"You are very perceptive. I can count on you to challenge our perspectives and bring well thought out solutions to the table."

"I notice that you are energized by learning new ideas and developing your skills. This allows you to thrive in our dynamic work environment."

"You are such a positive person; you are always looking for the constructive outcome in any situation and show up to work with a can-do attitude."

Employees who are seen, heard, and recognized make better employees. If acknowledging is left out of the coaching process, then all you're doing is working on the problems, while missing out on the opportunities to celebrate the authentic person who comes to work. Think of it as also focusing on the human "being" and not always on the human "doing."

FOCUS ON STRENGTHS

Find your employees' strengths and focus on how those strengths help them contribute to the business. By acknowledging your employees and their talents, the positive reinforcement then will result in their continuing to perform at a high level to keep receiving that wonderful appreciation. If they're doing a good job, then you're validating them by encouraging them to do more and perform at a higher level of effectiveness.

Each person comes to a job with goals, values, dreams, and a desire to make a difference. Through these conversations, you are not only acknowledging the person but you are creating a place where people feel valued, possibilities can be discovered and new perspectives can be more fully explored.

BE POSITIVE

One of the core ways to create forward motion and operate in your leadership sweet spot is to lead by example: remember to acknowledge yourself, your skills, talents and progress you're making. The way you think about yourself and the things you say to yourself will show up in all that you do and say to others. Is your self-talk positive and empowering, or is it negative and limiting? Find a way to start each day being inspired about what you can do. Be positive.

Create some inspiration for yourself and create a more

positive outlook to operate from each day. What would it take to be inspired by your work, and then to share that inspiration with others? If your goal is to make a difference with others, to find great satisfaction with their jobs and their time at work, then challenge yourself to be a leader who comes to work inspired, acknowledging the unique capabilities within yourself and your employees.

We can only be said to be alive in those moments when our hearts are conscious of our treasures.

—Playwright and Novelist Thornton Wilder

123

Conclusion

Win the talent war by becoming a

Coaching Leader

THE RECIPE FOR THE SECRET SAUCE IS NOW YOURS

In Texas, where I'm from, it seems that every family has a secret sauce for barbecue. And the recipe is often closely guarded. By now, you know that the secret sauce for finding your sweet spot is to become a coaching leader who is committed to the growth and development of your employees.

As a business coach, my work is tremendously rewarding: every day I get to help my clients find their leadership sweet spot. We use the formula you read about earlier:

Engage + Impact + Celebrate = Leadership Sweet Spot

I encourage you to make a commitment to yourself that *you* will find your sweet spot as a coaching leader.

Everyone I know who has found their leadership sweet spot did so by practicing over and over again on that one skill or right action that they so passionately wanted to achieve. My earliest memory of finding my "sweet spot" was in grade school, when I wanted to play the flute and to be the very best. How do you get to Carnegie Hall, I wondered – **practice, practice, practice**. So I practiced every day for hours. While I didn't make music my career, I was a soloist in my high school orchestra and moved on to playing the flute in my college orchestra as well.

If we want something badly enough we have to do what it takes to achieve our goals. I'm sure you have your own success story, one of accomplishment through determination and focused practice. To be a successful coaching leader takes tenacious effort and practice to master the skills that will make you the "best boss"—the boss people will appreciate and remember because you made a lasting impact on their lives.

Ernest Hemingway said, *"It is good to have an end to journey toward; but it's the journey that matters, in the end."* The journey from manager to coaching leader is one in which you can take small steps: you might begin by becoming a better listener. Learn to truly listen to your employees and watch the magic happen. When you've mastered the skill of listening, begin asking powerful questions. Next you can put those skills together for compelling conversations. Commit to using your new communications skills as a great listener and asking powerful questions to start coaching conversations and make a positive difference in the lives of your employees. You'll find your sweet spot as a coaching leader by creating breakthrough results for yourself, your company and your employees.

BRING THE COACHING TALENT SOLUTION™ TO YOUR WORKPLACE

While this book outlines the steps to develop coaching leadership skills, The Coaching Talent Solution™ program brings the techniques to life by teaching managers and leaders how to create meaningful impact and positive change in both themselves and their employees. By embracing the coaching approach in talent management, participants will learn how to adopt the mindset of a coaching leader and develop the coaching skills that will enhance employee performance, increase overall employee satisfaction and ultimately will increase the bottom line.

What you will discover through The Coaching Talent Solution™:

- How understanding the differences between managers and coaching leaders will help you with interactions with your peers, direct reports and even your supervisors.
- What to do to have your employees think of you as the best boss ever.
- The secret in turning average results from your employees into breakthrough outcomes for everyone.

- Learn how coaching leaders can overcome low employee engagement and finally enjoy a workplace with satisfied and productive followers.
- How you can use coaching to get promoted into your own dream job.
- Using the STAR Coaching Model - an incredibly simple process, to dramatically increase success with your team and for your organization.
- And.... you will have the secret to gain competitive advantage in the marketplace while attracting high performing employees to your team.

Once you have experienced the Coaching Talent Solution™, you will be able to create rewarding, challenging and compassionate relationships with loyal employees who can deliver extraordinary results. This program includes pre and post continuous learning aspects, which encourages personal transformation, skill development and confidence building while ensuring accountability and sustainability.

Acknowledgements

My sincere thanks to everyone who saw me through this book; I appreciate each of you, as I could not have taken on this project without you. You will forever be in my heart and have my gratitude. I'd like to especially thank the following people:

- My wonderful clients. I'm sure I've learned more from you than I could possibly have taught you.

- Mary Ann Copp, Pam Duffett, Valerie Taloni, EJ Rodgers, Rivka Willick, Bryce Winter and my CCI gang for graciously supporting me in my endeavors, the transitions of my life and for sharing your time and wisdom.

- My crazy and wacky family of origin, who—because of the values that I was taught as a child—brought me to the place of trying to make a difference in the lives of others.

- Jessica, William, and Lexi for helping me to recognize that being a mother is a beautiful journey of love. Last and not least, Mark, who makes the world a better place for me and who always provides his gentle guidance, support, and compassion.

About the Author

Known for her compassionate and truth-telling candor, Denise has coached and trained hundreds of executives and leaders since 2003. Whether working one-on-one with a client or as a team facilitator, Denise's commitment is to guide people to greater clarity about their vision. Her ability to quickly build trust and her partnering style creates an environment in which others can speak their truth and boldly move to a more purposeful life and career.

Denise earned a MBA in Human Resource Management from the University of Dallas. After working with several Fortune 500 companies as a manager and a leader, Denise pursued a coaching certification from the Hudson Institute of Santa Barbara; becoming an Executive Coach in 2003. She has over two decades of experience in coaching, consulting and facilitating learning experiences. Denise is certified by the International Coach Federation as a PCC (Professional Certified Coach).

Denise is currently an examiner for Columbia University's Coaching Certification Program and is committed to empowering others to create impact through Coaching. Denise has developed the Coaching Talent Solution^{TM}, a program that transforms the workplace by developing a sustainable culture of successful Coaching Leaders while improving profitability.

Contact the Author

Denise Henry welcomes your emails and phone calls.

Email: Denise@denisehenry.com

www.denisehenry.com